Forecasting Techniques in Business and Economics

Forecasting Techniques in Business and Economics

L. N. Dahiya

GYAN

ISBN: 978-81-212-1997-6

Published, 2020

Published by

Gyan Publishing House
5, Ansari Road
Daryaganj, New Delhi-110002
Phone: 011-47034999, 9811692060
www.gyanbooks.com
E-mail: books@gyanbooks.com

GYAN

Printed at: G. Print Process, Delhi.

To my Mother
Smt. Phoolan Wanti
who taught me so much about
self-reliance and
benevolence

Contents

Acknowledgements

I would like to thank all those who encouraged and made constructive comments in the execution of this book. My special gratitude to Prof. Dalip S Swamy, Professor and Head, Department of Business Economics, University of Delhi, who agreed to write a foreword for this book. I have been fortunate to receive the advice of many. Prof. A.K. Mathur of Jawahar Lal Nehru University, New Delhi, my Ph.D. supervisor, Prof. Vikas Mishra and Prof. S. Kaushil of Kurukshetra University, Prof. M. Saeed of Minot State University, USA, Prof. B.P. Singh, Delhi School of Economics, University of Delhi, Prof. J.D. Agarwal, Director, Indian Institute of Finance, New Delhi and Prof. Karam Pal Narwal, Director of HSB, G.J University of Science and Technology, Hisar, deserve special mention in this regard. I am also thankful to Smt. Sudershan Juneja, my previous publisher, for her cooperation in the production of the book in 1988. I am extremely grateful to Gyan Publishers, New Delhi for reproducing the book, with some changes, in an attractive design.

Rohtak **L.N. Dahiya**
June 2020

Foreword

Forecasting is a necessary step in the process of planning. The success of any enterprise depends upon the extent to which its executives are able to predict the demand and production as well as Government policies related to their products. The need for a good textbook on forecasting, therefore, cannot be overestimated.

The present book on forecasting through its four parts and seven chapters is welcome. It provides a comprehensive coverage of the subject matter in a coherent and systematic manner.

The book is unique in many respects. Firstly, it is written in a simple language and various techniques are lucidly explained. With a minimum of technical background a student can follow its exposition without much strain. Secondly, besides providing good theoretical discussion on more than two dozen forecasting techniques, the book contains solved illustrations to a variety of business and economic problems. It clarifies sets of rules and general guidelines for the forecaster to follow. The author has also neatly integrated the forecasting with planning and decision making. Similarly, the role of computer in the field of forecasting has also been highlighted. Thirdly, in one handy volume the author has condensed the essence of the subject matter without missing any important link and detail. In fact, Dr. L. N. Dahiya has used his experience of research and teaching at several universities. He has provided in the book just what is needed in the area and to my mind this is an important addition to the existing books on forecasting.

Fourthly, the book will be helpful in satisfying the requirement of post-graduate students of many disciplines. The present volume thus serves as a standard textbook on the subject. As it is complete and self contained, it will be quite useful to business executives, managers and others who deal with uncertain future while taking decisions.

In my opinion the book will be useful to those readers who practice and use forecasting as a tool for analysis.

Dr. Dalip S. Swamy
Professor,
Department of Business Economics
University of Delhi

Preface

Forecasting techniques are of vital importance to business managers, economists and others. Organizations of all sizes feel it essential to develop and use forecasts to reduce uncertainty and complexity of the business environment and to take maximum advantage of the opportunities available to them. Consequently, the past two decades have witnessed a number of developments in the field of forecasting. The recent developments in this field have been made possible due to the advent of computer technology and wide spread availability of programmable calculators. But unfortunately, there remained a gap between the theoretical formulation and practical application of forecasting methodologies. Not only this, there is a plethora of forecasting techniques the differences among of which are not always easy to comprehend making it very difficult to select an appropriate forecasting method suited to a particular situation.

The text stemmed from my being asked to give a course in business forecasting to M. Com. and M. Phil. (Commerce) students in the Faculty of Commerce and Business Management at the M. D. University, Rohtak. I soon became aware of the lack of suitable literature for meeting many of the needs of the students on the topic. And then I decided to make an attempt to write a text that I hope will provide a clear understanding and sufficient knowledge of the problem of forecasting for post-graduates in economics, business, commerce, management, operation research, production engineering and all others who are seeking means of improving their ability to plan for an uncertain future.

The book is designed to facilitate the applications of a variety of forecasting techniques and practical problems in a straightforward manner. Undue emphasis on mathematics is avoided and its level has been kept at the bare minimum. However, some basic knowledge of statistics is assumed.

The book is divided into Four Parts. Part One consists of first two Chapters. Chapter One is introductory in nature and presents an overview of forecasting. It describes the role and level of forecasting inter-alia. Chapter Two gives a bird-eye view of the existing forecasting techniques. The details of these techniques are discussed in later chapters.

Part Two and Part Three focus on quantitative and qualitative techniques of forecasting, respectively. Chapter Three through Chapter Four belonging to Part Two describe many different methods of forecasting commonly categorized as quantitative forecasting techniques. Chapters Five and Six which form Part Three of the book deal with a number of different qualitative technological forecasting methods and their applications in business and economics. Here, a selective approach has been adopted which does not attempt to explain every technique found in the literature of forecasting. The techniques covered here are those which are of greatest value. Finally, Part Four containing sole Chapter Seven describes how the forecasting function can be integrated into planning process. It also describes the process of selecting a forecasting method and data requirement suited to a particular problem. Besides, it also stresses the role of computer in the field of forecasting.

Towards the end of the book a comprehensive list of reading material in the field of forecasting has also been added. This I hope would prove very useful for managers and forecasters in carrying out further research in the field.

L.N. Dahiya

L.N. Dahiya

Rohtak

PART ONE

Part One has two chapters. Chapter One, 'Introduction', is intended to be used as a starting point for the analysis of forecasting. It underlines the need for a forecasting system in an organization. It is essential that in order to make forecasting programme a success, it should be effectively organized and co-ordinated. To achieve this objective it requires on the part of the forecaster a full understanding of the 'levels' of forecasting activity. Thus, forecasting organization with its 'levels' has been analyzed here. This approach will definitely help in making forecasting a more systematic, articulate, and methodological. There are many sets of rules and guidelines for the forecaster to follow for preparing a good and suitable forecast with limited resources. This requires skill and attributes of a good forecast analyst. All these related aspects of forecasting have also been adumbrated in this chapter.

Chapter Two brings out the elements essential for developing a comprehensive forecasting system. These elements are: quality, quantity, time and probability. The classification of elements would help and reinforce to clarify the forecaster's awareness on certain points to be considered while preparing forecast. Apart from these, this chapter provides a brief discussion on the wide range of forecasting techniques.

Chapter One

Introduction

1.1 The Growth of Forecasting

Forecasting is a process of predicting a value for future period on a systematic basis under certain assumptions and conditions. These predictions may be for a very near future, like the week, or the month ahead, or a distant future, like 5-10 or even more years hence.

Forecasting has received attention in the last fifteen years more than any other method of management. The word forecasting was rarely used prior to 1960s, although elementary methods like trend extrapolations were commonly used. It is only recently that attempts have been made to establish forecasting on a scientific basis. The main stimuli for the development of more scientific methods in the field occurred in the late 1960s. As a result, forecasting now is being widely used by economists and business managers to a variety of problems. Not only economists and business managers, but many scientists and engineers are also involved in the technique of forecasting in a technical capacity. So to say, forecasting has reached the stage at which it can be possible to perform management function more effectively. Until recently, forecasts made in business planning were more or less purely managerial guesses. But now there area wide variety of quantitative forecasting techniques which can be incorporated into a more formal forecasting system.

The factors responsible for the quick expansion in the application of forecasting particularly the quantitative methods are numerous which are described here:

(i) The greatest impact on forecasting was perhaps because of fast development and adoption of electronic computers. These computers have not only become widespread and readily available in many big organizations, but the cost aspect of such computers to use those in forecasting has improved substantially. It is now possible to store data with the help of computers. These data can also be retrieved when need arises for a new forecast. Fortunately, a new type of computer package has been developed in recent years that has been aimed specifically at the needs managers have for forecasting support. AH this has given a great outburst and proliferation of new techniques in forecasting.

(ii) The rapid growth of corporate sector and its systematic planning has highlighted the need for forecasting. The management structure has turned out to be a highly formalized and the element of uncertainty and complexity in business has necessitated the use of forecasting techniques. la fact, forecasting has become a matter of growth and survival for all kinds of organizations.

(iii) The rate of investment in industrial research has been increasing quite rapidly. The increased resources at the disposal of the forecaster have enabled him to make use of sophisticated quantitative forecasting techniques.

(iv) Use of mathematics in forecasting techniques to fit the varied situations has also made the forecasting system more attractive, precise and scientific. Correspondingly, there has also been the growth in expert personnel to handle these techniques effectively.

(v) On account of the sophisticated methods of forecasting that have been developed, the level of accuracy of forecasting has also increased tremendously. The result has been that now managers have started placing greater degree of confidence in the techniques of forecasting as an aid in decision making.

1.2 Levels of Forecasting

Forecasting is an important element for management in almost every type of activity. Forecasting is done at different levels. There are broadly two levels of forecasting as summarized below:

(i) *Macro Levels:* These provide insight into aggregate economic conditions such as level of Gross National Product (GNP), disposable income, total industrial production, population, employment, and so on. Econometric model of forecasting and Barometric forecasting are the most commonly used techniques at macro levels.

(ii) *Industry/Firm Level*: Industry forecasts are made for broad product groups. Sophisticated forecasting techniques often enable forecasters to generate quite accurate projections for rather specific products or items. The advantage of an industry level forecast is that the relative share of the firm in the whole industry can be determined. If industry data are either non-existent or too inaccurate to enable meaningful industry forecast to be generated then the product forecasts for the firm are often developed. The organizational level for collection of material and preparation of forecasts is generally at the level of the firm. Some examples where business forecasting do immense good to the firm are as under:

(a) Marketing : Forecastings are especially useful in the field of marketing. To determine whether

a company should expect an improved, static or declining market, it is necessary to forecast carefully the share of market, sales organizational estimates, customer sales trends etc. Marketing manager of the firm would also like to apply forecasting techniques for planning, advertising, pricing and promotion of the firm.

(b) *Production Scheduling and Inventory Control*: Forecasting makes it possible for the firms to plan production schedules and also the maintenance of inventories. It is necessary that each product line is predicted. The firm's demand forecast is used as input for production planning and for control of finished goods inventory. At the production planning stage, a monthly, and in some cases weekly, forecast for specific products such as specific models, sizes and so on, is required.

(c) *Process Control*: It is not possible to evolve a worthwhile system of process control without forecasting. It is useful in processing. For instance, if the process has become less efficient then forecasts of future behaviour can be used to plan the shutdown time and overhaul schedule.

(d) *Scheduling Existing Resources* : For the efficient use of resources, it requires the scheduling of production, transportation, cash, personnel, and so on. Forecasts of the level of demand for product, material labour, financing, or service are an essential input to such scheduling. Forecasting is also required to determine future resource requirements.

(e) *Personnel Management :* Forecasting is useful for planning the number of workers required in different job categories for recruiting and training programme.

(*f*) *Finance* : For acquiring capital investment it is absolutely necessary to predict the rate of interest which is the cost of capital.

1.3 Forecasting Organization

In order to make forecasting an effective tool, it is imperative to organize and co-ordinate it appropriately at all levels of responsibility. The number of responsibility levels varies from organization to organization. Table given below brings out the usual break down of responsibility levels for a firm which is engaged in manufacturing and selling of a consumer product :

Table 1.1 Forecasting Organization

Sr. No.	*Responsibility Level*	*Activities*
1.	Economist and Statistician	Analyze economy Analyze industry trends Determine share of market
2.	Forecaster	Forecast product lines Forecast end products
3.	Line managers and System analysts	Establish objectives Design system to explode forecast Identify limiting factors

It is evident from the Table given above that there are three well specified levels of responsibility for forecasting activities. At the first level of responsibility, economists with the help of statisticians study the impact of economic fluctuations on all economic and business activities of the concerned organization. The analysis thus carried out both by economists and statisticians would prove an input to forecaster. The responsibility of the forecaster at level two would be accomplished if he can provide an accurate time-phased forecast by end-product broken down by sales territory. At responsibility level three, the line managers and the system analysts then would determine as to what information is required from the forecasting system and design the information system needed to "explode" the input data from product lines and end products to provide timely action and evaluation reports that will satisfy the desired business objectives. They will also identify the limiting factors in implementing the forecast.

1.4 The Forecast Analyst

A qualified forecaster is genuinely needed for the organization. But the unfortunate situation is that in large number of companies there is no post of forecast analyst. Generally, a line manager performs this task on a part-time basis. Another approach which is currently in practice in many organizations is to hire an external consulting agency to perform the forecasting function. These ad hoc arrangements obviously cannot serve the organizations with continuity. Thus, a forecast analyst on full time basis, particularly for the sufficiently viable firm, is required appropriately.

As to the responsibilities of a forecast analyst, these are enormous at all operating levels. He should be fully qualified for the job and should be sharp and analytic in mind. The required skills and the qualifications for the forecast analyst can be listed as under :

(i) *Degree :* A forecaster is expected to know several subjects such as mathematics, economics, accounting or statistics. Thus, a degree in these branches is required. A master's degree or a doctor's would be even better. A person already holding this position in an organization should be imparted further training in the field of business, mathematics, algebra, calculus or statistics.

(ii) *Experience* : Some experience at different levels of management is desirable. It is better if the person has already been in the area of the uses of the forecasts. While recruiting, the persons possessing experience in inventory management, purchasing management, production planning, sales and distribution management should be preferred. It is worthwhile that the forecast analyst be exposed to a training in all the techniques of forecasting.

(iii) *Knowledge* : Once the person is selected for the job then he will have to acquire the minimum technical knowledge in the course of time. But this knowledge itself is not sufficient. He must have the sharpness of mind to learn through experiences rather than to possess simply a specific knowledge. A good judgement can only be possible through experience over the time period. Judgemental factor becomes more important than even the knowledge in the final analysis of the forecasting procedure.

(iv) *Other Qualities*: As indicated, forecast analyst should be sharp and should possess solution oriented mind. He should also be courageous enough so as to put this decision without any fear and pressure. He should be methodological in his approach. He should be self-confident and should possess, last of all, the required patience.

1.5 General Principles and Guidelines for a Forecaster

There are many sets of principles and guidelines for the forecasters which are briefly adduced below :

(i) *Economic Climate*: The forecaster will analyze the general economic conditions which are prevailing. Then he will link these with the problems in the organizations and industry. Once key indicators of the economy are determined and analyzed, it becomes easy to project future of an organization in terms of its sales, profits etc.

(ii) *Marketing Surveys* : Marketing surveys are useful in preparing a forecast. This is more so in case of new products and new sales territories. Through these surveys, the preferences of the customers can be known, and the product line can be developed accordingly. Perhaps it is the best way of getting information required for developing forecasts.

(iii) *Price Trends* : Forecaster must analyze the price trends very carefully. For instance, price affects both the volume of sales and level of profit. He should know how volume-price varies along with cost-unit with sales volume. For preparing such a type of relationship, i.e., price-volume-cost requires skill and experience on the part of the forecaster. Forecaster should evaluate customers, competitors and industry pricing practices judiciously for developing a good forecast.

(iv) *General Demand for Products* : The demand for the market is very important consideration in forecasting. Forecaster should evaluate all the factors which determine and affect the demand properly. For instance, in a declining market, forecaster must be realistic and should be satisfied even if present share of the company in the total demand is maintained. On the contrary, if the forecaster is optimistic about the demand situation in the market then he should be in a position to defend it with arguments and logic based on competitive analysis. He is also expected to review all potential and actual new products to determine whether they will be successful or not in the market.

(v) *Presentation of Results :* The results of the forecast should be presented in a form as are easily understood and put into practice towards solving clearly defined objectives. The objectives must be stated in quite unambiguous terms. It is also the duty of the forecaster to mention the risk involved in the adoption of a forecast so that management does not take decision and act in haste.

(vi) *Forecast in Range* : All agree on the point that forecasting is more or less a guess work. Once the forecasts are made, these are 10 be converted into practical management decision. It is the responsibility of the forecaster if estimates are void of the actual. So while recommending action, forecaster must express his figures in ranges to avoid this situation. For instance, in the matter of sales it is better to say that 20 percent chance of sales being under Rs. 20,000 or over Rs. 15,000 instead of giving one single figure say Rs. 17,500

(vii) *Apply Scientific Technique* : It is significant that relatively more scientific techiques of forecasting need to be applied. Only a scientific technique is capable of exploring in a better way cause-effect relationship between variables in an organization. For the application of such a technique, forecaster must possess an organized accumulation of knowledge of the organization.

(viii) *Suitability of Technique* : The choice of forecasting technique is largely based on the availability of data. The required facts must be available sufficiently in advance to generate a good forecast. If data is scanty and less suitable then a forecasting approach that can be developed with data limitations may be used.

(ix) *Use Historical Data with Caution* : As the business conditions are not stable and are in flux, it is risky to assume that past would reflect the future. It is the job of the forecaster to review change in conditions on a continuous basis and to incorporate these while developing forecast.

(x) *Less Expensive* : Forecasting cost is an important consideration particularly for the small organization. In those organizations where finance is the major constraint, it is advisable that forecaster tries simple and less complex forecasting techniques based on readily available data. No doubt, more complex approaches which require more funds have their own merits, but these should be tried and attempted only when required finance can easily be set aside by the organization for the purpose.

(xi) *Testing is Necessary* : Forecasting is not done only on papers, but it is to be put to test in the real situation. It is just possible that many forecasting theories when put to test are found awefully inadequate. It might also happen that forecasters are very good but may not be successful to make their forecast workable and operational. Thus, empirical testing is indispensable especially for the new forecasters. Continuous checking to see if the forecasting conclusions are valid or not should be a standard practice to be followed by the organization.

Chapter Two

Forecasting Elements and Techniques

Now we proceed to discuss through this chapter the elements of forecasting system, classification of forecasting techniques and also their brief description.

2.1 The Elements of a Forecasting System

There are four elements of a forecasting system. These elements are : quality, quantity, time and probability. All these elements are essential for a comprehensive forecasting system. The knowledge of these elements will help to resolve the basic difficulty of the forecaster in the matter of choosing an appropriate technique out of numerous available techniques.

Quality: The element of quality is a starting point for a comprehensive forecast. This element is followed in turn by three other elements which deal, respectively, with the dimensions of quantity, time and probability. Quality is the purely narrative of an event, a product or a process. Through this element, one seeks ideas that are useful in providing a basis for speculation and new insights. Here forecaster makes the best use of his intuition and memory. This is an essential element, as pointed out earlier, and without which other elements become meaningless. Techniques of forecasting which ignore this element and include only three viz., quantity, time and probability are valueless in themselves.

Quantity : Quantitative element describes the level of activity of the concept measured in well defined terms or units. It is absolutely necessary for comprehensive forecasting to acquire the quantitative data. To be more explicit, there is a need in forecasting to determine the basic attribute which adequately represents the phenomenon being forecast. The word 'attribute' is used to describe the particular characteristics or property on which the forecast is based. An attribute which is quantified is said to have a 'parameter'—a well defined unit which measures the attribute. In economics, for example, the indices of Gross National Product (GNP) and per capita are obviously the readily definable criteria by which to measure economic attributes. The time series techniques are the most frequently used means for determining this element.

Time : The time element of a forecast needs to be expressed clearly usually in terms of a date. There is a close association between the quantitative and the time elements of a forecast and follows a regular pattern. Thus, a forecaster has a basis for extrapolating these past trends into the future. This provides the rationale for a range of time series forecasting techniques. We may have simple time series which is represented by a straight line or a curve, frequently exponential fitted to historical data. But growth is not an unending process which will approach a limit. This has led to the development of very useful concept of the Growth or 'S' curve which can be expressed mathematically as Logistic or Gompertz curve. There are many situations which conform to 'S' type growth. Dynamic modeling, which expresses mathematically causal relationship between all the factors influencing the development of a technology, is also largely directed towards forecasting the time element.

Probability : This is the fourth element of a comprehensive forecasting system. This element ensures that no factor which could affect the forecast is ignored. Probability in forecasting means some statement of the chance or likelihood of an event. The value of probability may be expressed in statistical terms of 0.0 to 1.0, or as percentage. However, there are a few ways of assessing probability. Delphi technique of forecasting, in spite of some defects, is the most convenient source of probability estimates and hence explains its popularity. But there is subjectivity involved in all techniques of assessing probability and this understandably leads to reduced confidence in this type of forecast. The problem is also aggravated further by the fact that there may be a chain-like sequence of events, and to assign probability value of all these turns out to be very difficult task. So, in practice, the forecaster faces an extremely difficult task due to multitude of highly diverse influencing factors and outcomes while generating a forecast by incorporating this element of probability.

We have mentioned above the various elements of forecasting. It is to be emphasized here that all elements are important and are needed for comprehensive forecasting. But the fact that it may not always be possible to prepare forecasts with all the stated dimensions is also to be admitted. Nevertheless, a forecaster should make a sincere attempt to consider all these elements by the most systematic means possible. A forecast which lacks one or other of the elements would obviously be a weak attempt. And it would be less helpful and useful as an input to any decision-making process.

2.2 Forecasting Techniques

A wide variety of forecasting techniques has been developed during the last two and a half decades. These range from the most naive techniques to highly complex ones. All these techniques can be classified in two broad types: (A) Quantitative and (B) Qualitative forecasting techniques.

(A) *Quantitative Techniques*: All quantitative forecasting techniques involve the analysis of historical data in an attempt to predict future values of a variable of interest. Some of the more widely used techniques in this category include exponential smoothing, decomposition and regression techniques. These techniques have come in acceptance largely because of the following factors.

(i) They develop record of accuracy for preparing new line forecasts.

(ii) Development and adoption of computers.

(iii) Generally less costly to prepare.

Quantitative forecasting techniques can further be classified into two main groups (a) Time Series and (b) Causal Techniques. A third category which is generally a mixture of (a) and (b) types is also possible to consider under the head "Others" (see Table 2 1).

(A) TIME SERIES: In the time series techniques, prediction of the future is based on past values of a variable. Then assuming that it will continue in the future, this pattern is extrapolated in order to generate forecast. Thus, time series forecasting models are most useful when conditions are expected to remain stable. The most widely used types of time series models are: Simple Exponential Smoothing and Decomposition.

(B) CAUSAL TECHNIQUES: Causal techniques, on the other hand, involve the identification of other variables related to the variables to be predicted and the factor to be forecasted which exhibit a cause-effect relationship with one or more independent variables. For instance, Sales = f (prices, income, competition etc.). On the basis of cause-effect relationship, a model is developed that describes the relationship between these variables and the variables to be predicted. The main types of Causal models are: Multiple Regression, Econometrics and Multivariate Box-Jenkins.

It is to be noted here that in order to apply all quantitative techniques, following three conditions should exist:

(i) Information about the past is available.

(ii) This information can be quantified in the form of numerical data.

(iii) It should be possible to assume that same features of the past pattern will also continue into the future, i.e., the assumption of continuity.

(B) *Qualitative Techniques*: Qualitative techniques involve the opinion of experts to predict future events subjectively. Qualitative techniques are also sometimes referred to as technological forecasting. The term technological forecasting may not sound proper substitute for qualitative techniques as the latter can be used to forecast several things other than technological developments. But the term has come to stay and is commonly used.

It is notable that qualitative techniques require different set of data than the quantitative forecasting techniques. There are situations where no quantitative information is available obviating the application of quantitative techniques. Under the circumstances, when quantitative information is not available but sufficient qualitative knowledge exists then qualitative techniques are to be used. For example, predicting the speed of transportation around the year 2,000, predicting how automobiles will look like in the year 2,010, the discovery of a new and very cheap form of energy that produces no pollution are some such situations. The solutions to these problems requirc inputs from a number of trained experts in the fields who have acquired the best understanding of the situation and also its evolution.

Qualitative techniques like quantitative techniques can be subdivided into two categories.

(a) Subjective Assessment Techniques

(b) Technological Forecasting Techniques

(a) SUBJECTIVE ASSESSMENT TECHNIQUES: This approach is used when there is presence of uncertainty concerning one or more of the relevant factors. The important techniques which fall under this category are : Jury of executive opinion, sales-force composite techniques, individual subjective probability assessment etc. Forecasts based on subjectivity require the use of statistical model. Generally, this model is referred to as Bayesian statistics or Bayesian analysis.

(b) TECHNOLOGICAL FORECASTING TECHNIQUES: The term 'Technological Forecasting' (TF) came into prominence in the early 1960s. This was a time when there was supreme confidence in the ability of technology to solve the majority of the world's economic and social problems. It is not surprising, therefore, that the need for forecasting technology was appreciated greatly. Technological approaches to forecasting can further be divided into following two categories.

(i) Explorative Techniques of Technological Forecasting

(ii) Normative Approaches to Technological Forecasting

In explorative techniques, current assured knowledge is made the basis to assess the conditions of the future. This includes several techniques like Scenario development technique, the Delphi technique, Morphological research etc. In normative forecasting techniques, the procedure to start with assessing future goals, needs, desires, objectives, etc. work backward to determine necessary developments in the area of interest. The popular approaches belonging to this category are Relevance trees, and Systems dynamics.

It may be mentioned that qualitative techniques are used chiefly to provide hints to aid the planners and to supplement quantitative forecasts. These techniques are mostly used by large companies for cost consideration and are used for medium and long range situations like formulating strategies, developing new product etc. It is to be admitted tbat Qualitative Forecasting Techniques are not as well developed as the Quantitative Forecasting Techniques. These are still mainly intuitive and their acceptance in industry is of recent origin.

The following Table summarizes the above mentioned categorization scheme of forecasting techniques:

Table 2.1: Classification of Forecasting Techniques

Broad Classification	*Nome of Technique*
(A) Quantitative Techniques	
(a) Time Series	(i) Naive Technique (ii) Smoothing Techiques The Mean Single Moving Averages Double Moving Averages Single Exponential Smoothing Double Exponential Smoothing Triple Exponential Smoothing Other Smoothing Techniques (iii) Decomposition Techniques Trend Fitting The Ratio-to Moving Averages Centered Moving Averages The Census II Decomposition Technique
(b) Causal or Explanatory	(i) Simple Regression (ii) Multiple Regression (iii) Econometric Models (iv) Input-Output Analysis
(c) Others	(i) The Box-Jenkins Forecasting (ii) Barometric Forecasting (iii) Cycle Forecasting
(B) Qualitative Techniques	
(a) Subjective	(i) Jury of Executive Opinion (ii) Sales Force Polling Technique (iii) Formal Survey and Market Research Based Assessment (iv) Individual Subjective Porbability Assessment

(*Contd...*)

(b) Technological	(i) Explorative Scenario Techniques The Delphi Approach Curve Fitting Analogy Morphological Research Gap Analysis (ii) Normative Relevance Trees Systems Dynamics

This Table gives a full range of forecasting techniques currently available. There are many factors to be considered while making an explicit selection of a particular methodology to be used. This requires much more detailed analysis and will be taken up in the next several chapters. Before we embark upon such detailed discussion, in respect of each technique, several important techniques of forecasting are reviewed in nut-shell for acquiring preliminary knowledge.

2.3 An Overview of Forecasting Techniques

Naive Technique: Naive technique is one of the simplest techniques. According to this technique, the most recent observed value in a series serves as a forecast value. For example, if the sales volume of a product for the coming week is to be forecasted, the observed value for the most recent week would be the forecast value. If the series exhibit seasonal fluctuations then data is to be adjusted for its seasonality. This naive technique of forecasting though quite artless and amusingly simple may provide very good results under certain situations.

Moving Average : This technique of forecasting helps in reducing the impact of randomness in the series. The element of randomness may be very significant, particularly when the time horizon for forecasting is very short. In order to minimize the randomness, an average of several of the past values is taken. As each new observation becomes available a new average can be computed by dropping the oldest observation and including the newest one. The procedure is termed as moving average. This moving average value will then be the forecast for the next period.

Simple Exponential Smoothing : Exponential smoothing is another technique that has become quite popular. This technique is quite similar to the Moving Average technique. But it does not use a constant set of weights for the most recent observations. Instead, an exponentially decreasing set of weights is used. This is done so that most recent values receive more weight than older values. This technique is found to be very useful and, in fact, is the only acceptable technique when forecasts are needed for thousand of items, as in case of many inventory systems. Since the technique is quite automatic, so there is no need of skilled manpower in its operation. The basic calculations involved are also quite straightforward. This technique is widely used for immediate and short-term forecasting.

Decomposition : Under this technique, data series is broken down (decomposed) into sub-patterns that identify each component of the time series separately. Such a break down can facilitate improved accuracy in forecasting. It would also help in understanding well the behaviour of the series. This is very effective technique of forecasting in dealing with cyclical components. This measures the seasonal component in terms of seasonal indices, which can be used to de-seasoualize the data. The technique undoubtedly is easy to understand, easy to use and also easy to interpret, but the chief disadvantage of this technique is that it is arbitrary in nature and suffers from theoretical weakness from a statistical point of view.

Barometric Forecasting : The barometric or leading indicating forecasting model is used primarily to identify potential future changes in general business conditions, rather than conditions for a specific industry or firm. The technique is based largely on the work done at the National

Bureau of Economic Research by Burns, Moore, Shiskin and Mitchell. Economic indicators may be classified as leading, coincident, or lagging indicators so that they represent commitments to future levels of economic activity. It must be made clear that the main value of leading and lagging indicators lies in predicting the direction of future change in economic activity. The technique, no doubt, is useful but also not without weaknesses. However, in order to cope with some of the weaknesses of the forecasting based on leading series, the device of diffusion index is applied which reduces the chances of making a false prediction based on a short-term fluctuations in one series alone. Diffusion index may be constructed using any combination of indicator series which the forecaster feels is appropriate.

Box-Jenkins (ARIMA) : Professors Box and Jenkins in their book entitled *Time Series Approach Analysis, Forecasting, and Control* gave an approach to short term forecasting which derives its name after the authors. This is also known as Autoregressive Integrated Moving Average (ARIMA) Technique. An ARIMA model is one that includes in its weighted terms both past values of the variables to be forecast and past values of the forecast errors. Through Box-Jenkins approach, it is possible to search for the relationship that best describes movements in time series, by using only past monthly values of a particular time series. The main advantage of the technique is that it allows for wide range of possible models for the data and provides a strategy for selecting a model from the class which best represents the data.

It may, however, be mentioned that this approach can be used only for series that are stationary, that is, series that do not have a long term trend. Another main limitation of the model is that it is costly in terms of computer time. This is why the approach has until recently been used by a very few business forecasters. It requires a sophisticated technical background which is necessary for its understanding. However, it is expected that as management becomes more sophisticated, the highly precise Box-Jenkins technique will be more widely used for immediate and short-term forecasts.

Regression Model Forecasting : Time series models cannot be used to predict the impact of changes in management policies, e.g., to predict the impact that price increase will have on the sales of a product. Regression model helps in attempting this by relating dependent variable to the number of independent variables. Whether simple or multiple regression is to be used would depend on the number of variables and the type of problem in hand. Generally, it is the Multiple Regression which is used as it allows one to determine the causal relationship between several variables and the items being forecast. This facilitates a better understanding of the situation and allows experimentation with different combinations of inputs to study their effects on the forecasts.

Econometric : Econometric Technique of forecasting is a combination of economic theory, mathematics and statistics to analyze economic and business relationships. Econometric model of forecasting may be of single or multiple equations. The inherent assumption in regression model that the independent variables are not affected by changes in the dependent variables is often unrealistic. Econometric models remove this flaw and enables the forecaster to take into account the simultaneous interaction between dependent and independent variables. One of the chief advantages of an econometric model is that values for several of the independent variables can be determined within the model. But these models are not without faults. The main disadvantage this model suffers from is that it is often rather complex and lengthy. The given technique is also quite expensive and costly. Besides, the development and specification of an econometric model requires the artificial application of statistical technique. Another disadvantage of this technique is that it requires forecasts of future values of the independent variables in the regression equation.

Input-Output Technique : Input-Output technique is a powerful and versatile tool for use in economic forecasting. The technique based on Leontief's input-output tables is quite sophisticated. Input-output model permits the forecaster to trace the measurement of the effects of all the demands (both direct and indirect) on the output of each industry influenced by an initial change in some final demand. In other words, it gives a total picture of the market for any group of commodities. However, the major weakness of the technique is that the construction of these input-output tables is a massive undertaking.

Jury of Executive Opinion : It is one of the simplest and most widely used forecasting approaches available. The subjective views of top management are averaged to generate future figures for the items to be forecast. Usually, this technique like survey and opinion polling technique is used in conjunction with some quantitative technique, such as trend extrapolation. The management jury then modifies the resulting forecast based on their own expectations and insights regarding that item. The major advantage of this approach is that it generates forecasts quickly and easily.

Formal Survey and Market Research Based Assessment: This technique is particularly useful in making short period forecasts. Through this technique, certain attitudes of the persons (sample), having an impact on economic and business decisions, may be identified in advance of the actual implementation of the decision. This technique is mostly used to supplement the other quantitative forecasting techniques The chief advantage of this technique is that it helps to understand changes in past relationships which the qualitative techniques assume will remain constant. Besides, these techniques provide the only source of data for estimating the demand for new product. However, skill is required in designing market research study that will discover such relationships and determine their validity.

The Delphi Approach : The Delphi approach is the most commonly used of technological or qualitative forecasting techniques. This is purely an opinion taking process from a group. The underlying objective is to procure a reliable consensus of opinion from a group of experts that can be used as a future forecast. However, these experts are kept apart so that their judgement is not influenced by social pressure or by other aspects of small group behaviour.

S-Curve Approach : The procedure for approximating an S-Curve is similar to that for a simple time series with the additional factor of finding the limiting level. The physical limit, however, relates to a specific technology. An S-Curve implies a slow start, a steep growth, and then a plateau. The shape of this curve is often used in depicting the product life cycle. However, the major problem in the use of S-Curve is to find the most appropriate type. It depends on the technology or the product one wants to forecast.

Analogy Technique : The concept is that when two things have been seen to have at least one characteristic in common, we tend to conclude that an analogy exists. Analogies are attempted to compare historical patterns with existing situations in order to forecast future programme and developments. These forecasts are generally technological in nature and involve changes in various technologies. There are several kinds of analogies like growth analogy, historical analogy, social and physical analogy which can be drawn.

Morphology : Morphology is the most systematic technique particularly for forecasting new products or new processes. This technique was developed by Zwicky, the Swiss astronomer in his attempts to discover new inventions in the field of jet engines. Morphological research is concerned with the development and the practical application of basic techniques that will analyze the structural inter-relationships among objects or phenomena. Thus, Morphological technique goes beyond simple forecasting applications and represents an approach to systematic thinking and problem solving. One of the basic advantages of the technique is that it allows the forecaster to identify hidden opportunities for technological possibilities that can be developed profitably.

Relevance Trees : In many types of problems adaptations, the relevance trees technique has found wide-spread application. Its origin dates back to the development of decision theory and the construction of decision trees which help the decision makers in selecting the best strategy from among a number of alternatives. The purpose of a relevance tree is to enable the decision maker to assess systematically the totality of all the interlocking technologies and tasks which could lead to the achievement of an objective and to select the most appropriate path. It should be realized that the cost of applying this technique can be quite substantial as it involves considerable human and computer resources. Therefore, the usefulness of the technique should always be weighed against its cost.

PART TWO

Part Two consisting of Chapters Three and Four is about the exposition of quantitative techniques of forecasting. The practical applications of these techniques have also been illustrated where-ever possible and essential. All quantitative techniques have been classified into two categories viz., Smoothing and Decomposition Time Series techniques, and Causal or Explanatory techniques. A third category of forecasting techniques which tends to include both time and causal elements has also been added under the bead "Others".

Smoothing techniques which are based on historical data are found to be quite appealing as these are easy to comprehend, easy to use and also less expensive. With the help of these techniques, the randomness in data is eliminated. As a consequence, the data pattern can be projected into the future which can be used for generating a forecast. Many such forecasting techniques have been attempted in Chapter Three.

Decomposition techniques which have also been described in the same chapter, approach to the problem of forecasting somewhat differently, as compared to smoothing techniques. The purpose of decomposition is to breakdown the pattern of time series into sub-patterns so that each component of the time series, such as seasonal, cycle and trend is identified. After obtaining separate sub-patterns of the series in terms of components these are then combined into a final forecast. Obviously, no such procedure is followed in case of smoothing technique which gives one single pattern of the time series.

Chapter Four belonging to this Part describes some causal or explanatory techniques of forecasting which are substantially different from the techniques discussed in Chapter Three. The Causal or Explanatory techniques which have found place in the text are: Regression technique, econometric technique and input-output technique. Regression technique attempts to predict the future describing and measuring the effect of important independent variables on the dependent variable to be forecast. Econometric model is just the extension of the multiple regression model. Some other important techniques like Box-Jenkins (ARIMA) and Barometric techniques have also been included though briefly in it. Box-Jenkins technique is very complex. And its widespread adoption gets hindered on account of the complexity. It is to be made clear here that the objective of this Part, which describes various forecasting techniques, is not to furnish all their statistical or mathematical details but to explain their use in a practical sense.

Chapter Three

Quantitative Forecasting Techniques—I (Naive Smoothing and Decomposition Time Series Techniques)

This chapter is concerned with Naive, Smoothing, and Decomposition forecasting techniques of the time-series in that order. These are the simplest possible models of time-series forecasting and can be used in a wide range of short term-forecasting situations. These techniques are particularly attractive when a large number of items are to be forecasted as in many inventory situations. Although these forecasting techniques are non-statistical in nature but have been accepted very well by the users for their simplicity and their low cost.

3.1 Naive Techniques

A forecasting technique is termed naive when it is not based on rigid theoretical considerations. Naive techniques can be classified into two categories viz., Naive (i) and Naive (ii).

Naive (*i*): In its simplest form, the naive (i) forecasting model assumes that historical values of some variable provide the best basis for estimating current or future values of that variable. Let the forecast value of the variable be denoted by S, X denotes an actual observed value of the variable, and the subscript (t) identifies the time period. Then the model would be:

$$S_{t+1} = X_t$$

Where S_{t+1} = the forecast for period $t+1$

X_t = the observed value in period t

which means that the forecast value of the variable for the next period will be the same as the value of that variable for the present period. As is clear, this type of model is quite easy to understand and to use. It is particularly useful for forecasting over short periods when there are no dramatic short-run changes in the data. In order to explain this method, following example has been given:

Table 3.1: Sales Forecast of Commodity 'X'

Week	*Sales (Rs. 000)*	*Forecast (Rs. 000)*
	X_t	S_t
1	7	—
2	8	7
3	7	8
4	8	7
5	7	8
6	9	7
7	8	9
8	7	8
9	9	7
10	—	9

In the above case, simple rule of forecasting has been followed. The rule is that the observed value of sales of commodity 'X' for the most recent week would be the forecast for the next week. Thus, the sales forecast for the 10th week would be 9 (000s) as was during the 9th week the most recent week. Alternatively stated, preceding's week sales are the forecast sales for the current week.

This technique evidently is artless and quite simple. But its utility diminishes greatly as it is based on the popular assumption that things will not change and the future events will resemble the present. For instance, sales of the next week will increase by the same amount as they did in the last week. This type of prediction acceptedly may be valid for most short term decisions, but it becomes more questionable as the period of forecast becomes larger. And, obviously, the assumption that the future is just the extension of the past, will not hold good in the long run.

Another basic limitation of such a model is the non-availability of required data for generating this type of forecast. Since the forecast of next week's sales requires that we know this week's sales, the forecaster may be faced with the task of collection of actual data with great speed. Besides, this technique is also beset with the problem, as it makes no provision for incorporating the effects of known changes of the factors which may affect sales. For example, monthly sales due to seasonality factor may understate or overstate the actual sales. On account of these drawbacks, the model becomes conditional and is to be used only when the value of the variable in question is relatively stable and exhibits slow and/or uniform pattern in data. But many practical business problems do not conform to this uniform trend in data and thus somewhat complex analysis of forecasting is required. To be more realistic, the data is to be adjusted for forecasting purpose in terms of their components namely secular, cyclical, seasonal and other random factors.

Naive (ii) : This is relatively a more sophisticated technique of forecasting as compared with Naive (i). As mentioned above, of the various components of time series, seasonality is one of the important factors. Under the Naive (ii), deseasonalization of the most recent observations is made and then it is reseasonalized for the period that is to be forecast. The predictive power of forecasting is greatly enhanced by introducing seasonal variations. These seasonal variations can be estimated in a number of ways. The best known of these techniques is the "ratio to trend technique." And through this technique it is possible to adjust the forecast figure for seasonally. This will be attempted further in this chapter. Naive (ii) which goes beyond Naive (i) considers thus the possibility of seasonally in the series. In other words, seasonally is removed from the original data for obtaining seasonally adjusted data under this forecasting system.

Acceptedly, the introduction of seasonality into a forecasting model should significantly improve the model's ability to predict. But their utility is limited to some extent as these do not seek to relate changes in a data series to the causes underlying observed values in the series. They would give very poor results when causal factors have undergone a change.

3.2 Smoothing Techniques

We have seen already that naive techniques will produce a forecast that will vary considerably because of the randomness in series. In order to eliminate the randomness in series, it is better to consider some kind of average of recent observed values. This has now been attempted. Here the aim is to present some kinds of averaging techniques for generating forecast. Such procedures are commonly known as smoothing techniqiues. The basis of the smoothing techniques described here is the simple weighting or smoothing of past observations in a time series for obtaining a forecast for the future. In the process of smoothing of the data values, random errors are got averaged giving a "smooth" forecast that suits well in certain situations. These techniques have several attractions, for they involve low cost and can be used and adopted readily. We will discuss in this chapter the most commonly used techniques of smoothing. It will be quite useful to classify smoothing techniques further. Smoothing techniques can be classified broadly into two groups namely, averaging techniques and exponential smoothing techniques. In averaging classification, we have simple average, (the mean), single (simple) moving average, double moving average and also various other moving averages. Our analysis, however, would be restricted only to the discussion of the first three techniques.

The second classification of exponential smoothing techniques includes single exponential smoothing, double exponential smoothing, triple exponential smoothing suggested by Brown and Winters and exponential smoothing given by Pegels. We shall, however, analyze only the first technique, i.e., single exponential smoothing to give an idea about the practical utility of this technique. It is not possible to discuss all the techniques that lie beyond the scope of this book.

The basic difference between the averaging techniques and exponential is that the former assign equal weights to all the observations whereas the latter apply to an unequal set of weights to the past observations. As the weights characteristically decrease in an exponential manner from the most recent to the most distant data point, the techniques are termed as exponential smoothing techniques.

3.2.1 Simple Average (The Mean) : This is quite a straight-forward technique. Under this technique, simple average of all the past data is taken as the forecast for period $t + 1$. The question to be asked is whether this simple technique is adequate for forecasting? The answer is both in affirmative and negative. This technique gives good result when there is no noticeable trend and no seasonality involved in the data. This is when the process is stationary. But this type of data behaviour is not exhibited by most business and other problems. When the data undergo sudden change, then the mean value used as forecast for the next period may not catch up, and cannot serve as forecast for the period under consideration.

3.2.2 Single (Simple) Moving Average : Moving average is the procedure of computing the average by leaving the oldest observation and including the newest one. This is a very simple way of reducing the flaw inherent in the single mean as forecast, as discussed earlier. The number of periods to be used in the moving average will be governed by several other considerations. It should, however, be remembered that the number of data points in each average remains constant Table 3.2 below gives the forecast of item 'AT' in terms of moving average.

Table 3.2: Forecasting the Demand for Item 'X' One Month Ahead by Using Moving Average.

1 *Month*	2 *Time Period*	3 *Observed Value (Units)*	4 *Three-Month Moving Average (Units)*
Jan.	1	100	—
Feb.	2	105	—
Mar.	3	110	—
Apr.	4	100	105
May	5	90	105
June	6	95	100
July	7	102	95
Aug.	8	104	95.67
Sept.	9	95	100.33
Oct.	10	107	100.33
Nov.	11	105	102
Dec.	12	—	102.33

The Table above illustrates the application of the technique of single moving average using three-month moving average for forecasting. In this Table the forecast values in column 4 are based on the values for the previous three months. For instance, the forecast for April is taken to be the average of three months viz., January, February and March Similarly, forecast values for other months can be computed by deleting the oldest value and including the newest one. Thus the last figure of 102.33 in column 4 is December's forecast and is the average for the months of September, October and November.

The forecasting figures can also be shown along with the observed figures diagrammatically. This will help further to show the accuracy of this technique. These values have been plotted on the graph and are given in Figure 3.1.

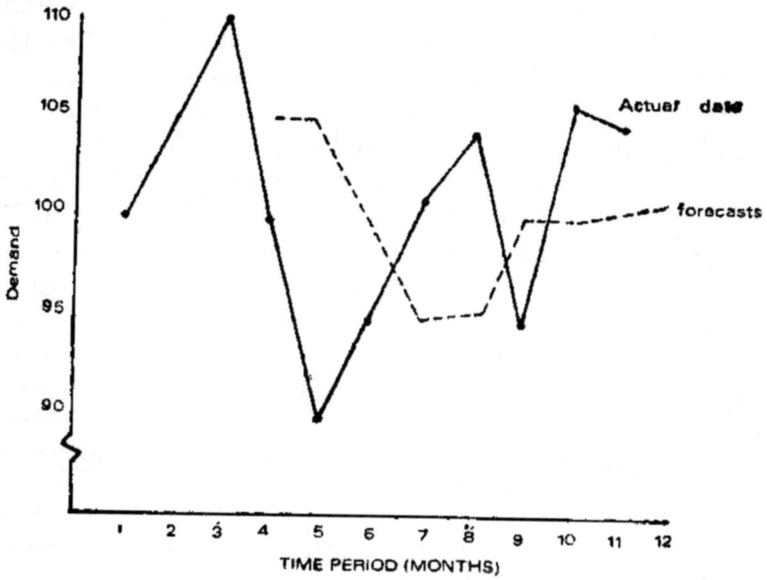

Fig. 3.1. Forecast for Demand of 'x'

This technique of forecasting is superior to the earlier technique of simple average on certain counts. But it does not mean that it is without faults. It has got its own limitations which should frankly be admitted at this stage. Firstly, it cannot handle trend or seasonality, adequately. Secondly, this technique can be used only in short term situations where pattern of data can be assumed to be more or less stable. Thirdly, it requires more storage of data as it needs data at different points and not just the average. For all these reasons, moving average as a forecasting technique is not generally practised in comparison with exponential technique which is another important smoothing forecasting technique.

3 2.3 *Double Moving Averages* : Simple moving average gives good result when the historical data exhibit a

horizontal pattern. This technique is unable to cope with trends or other complex patterns of data. Therefore, higher form of smoothing is required to handle such data. Double moving average is one such smoothing technique to cope with this situation.

Double moving average is a moving average of a moving average. The procedure of forecasting with the double moving average is described here and the results are presented in Table 3.3. In the first step, simple moving average of the observed data is computed. Then in the next step, moving average of the moving average, already worked out, is computed. Thirdly, the difference between the single moving average and the double moving average is counted and is added back to the single moving average (col. 5). Next, in order to make this technique more exact an adjustment factor is computed (column 6). The technique of adjustment (column 6) is elaborated further. Finally, the "actual forecast is presented (col. 7).

Table 3.3 contains the results of applying double moving averages to the forecasting. In mathematical terms the forecast developed in Table 3.3 may be summarised as under :

$$\text{Column 3} \quad S'_t = \frac{X_t + X_{t-1} + X_{t-2} + \ldots + X_{t-N+1}}{N},$$

$$\text{Column 4} \quad S''_t = \frac{S'_t + S'_{t-1} + S'_{t-2} + \ldots S'_{t-N+1}}{N},$$

$$\text{Column 5} \quad a_t = 2\,S'_t - S''_t\,,$$

$$\text{Column 6} \quad b_t = \frac{2}{N-1}(S'_t - S''_t),$$

$$\text{Column 7} \quad S_{t+m} = a_t + b_t m,$$

where $N = 3$ and $m = 1$ in the example

S = Single moving average,

S'_t = **Single moving average,**

S''_t = **Double moving average,**

S'_{t+m} = **the forecast in periods in advance,**

b_t = **the adjustment to the forecast at time t.**

Note that b_t involves a factor $2/N - 1$.

Table 3.3: Forecasting A Series With Double Moving Average

1 *Time Period*	2 *Actual Value*	3 *Three Month Single Moving Average*	4 *Three Month Double Moving Average*	5 *Value of a*	6 *Value of b*	7 *Forecast Value (a + bm when m = 1)*
1	2					
2	4					
3	6	4				
4	8	6				
5	10	8	6	10	+2	
6	12	10	8	12	+2	12
7	14	12	10	14	+2	14
8	16	14	12	16	+2	16
9	18	16	14	18	+2	18
10	20	18	16	20	+2	20
11	—	—	—	—	—	22

It is to be noted that forecasting one period (m = 1) in advance, forecast is simply the sum of columns 5 and 6. For two periods in advance the forecast would be column 5 plus twice column 6, and so on. For instance, the forecast for period 12, given that $t = 10$ would be 20 + 2(2) = 24.

3.2.4 *Exponential Smoothing Technique:* We are already aware that there are some severe limitations and drawbacks of the moving average techniques. The first major limitation of these techniques had been the requirement to store the last N observed values. This process is quite expensive. Another drawback which is associated with these techniques is to assign equal weights to each of the last N observations and no weight at all to observations before period $(t - N)$. It is not logical to assign equal weights to all the observations. Actually, more weight should be assigned to recent observations as they provide information about what will happen in the future. This procedure to assign more weights to relatively recent observations is being followed by the technique of exponential smoothing. In other words, it is the procedure of forecasting where decreasing weights are assigned to the older observations.

The technique of exponential smoothing was introduced by Holt and Brown in 1956-57. Since that time, the concept of exponential smoothing has grown and become a practical technique with wide applications, particularly in the forecasting of inventories and sales. The exponential smoothing technique which is a special kind of weighted moving average has now come to stay a very popular short term forecasting technique.

The exponential smoothing technique tends to eliminate randomness in the historical observations, but the mathematical procedure used for smoothing is somewhat different from that used in the case of moving averages. The simple case of single exponential smoothing can be developed from the equation given below:

$$S_{t+1} = S_t + \alpha(X_t - S_t) \qquad (3.1)$$

where S_t = preceding forecasting figure or the forecasting for time *t*,

X_t = observed value at time *t* corresponding to the preceding forecasting figure,

α = is a weighting factor whose value ranges between 0 to 1.

With given value of α (alpha), weights to past observations can be assigned. These weights decrease exponentially hence the name exponential smoothing. In fact α is used to smooth past values of the data and errors in forecast. For example, if alpha is = .2 then it would assign weights = .2, to the last present observation (X_t)

and this weight to the preceding observation (X_t — 1) would be α (1 — α) = .16, α (1 — α)^2 = .128, and so on.

The application of single exponential smoothing can be illustrated with the following table giving a hypothetical series of annual sales of commodity 'X'

Table 3.4: Forecasting the Sales of 'X' one month ahead using Exponential Smoothing

Month	*Time Period*	*Observed Values*	*Exponentially* α = .2	*Smoothed Values* α = .5	α = .9
Jan.	1	100	—	—	—
Feb.	2	90	100 00	100.00	100.00
Mar.	3	105	98.00	95 00	91.00
Apr.	4	110	99.40	100.00	103.60
May	5	85	101.52	105.00	109.36
June	6	95	98.22	95.00	87.44
July	7	102	97.58	95.00	94.25
Aug.	8	104	98.46	98.50	101.23
Sept.	9	94	99.57	101.25	103.49
Oct.	10	92	98.46	97.62	94.95
Nov.	11	100	97.17	94.81	92.29
Dec.	12	—	97.74	97.41	99.23

Table 3.4 gives the forecasted values of 'X' with given values of alpha .2, .5, and .9 respectively. The values for the last three columns have been computed by using tbe equation (3.1). It is to be noted that there is no forecast for the first period as there is no earlier forecast. In fact, there is problem of initialization of the first forecast. How to go about it? There are two ways of doing it. First procedure could be to use the first observed value (X_1) as the first forecast and then apply the technique by using the equation (3.1). Second procedure would be to take average of the first three or four observations in the data set and use it as the initial forecast. Reverting to the computation of forecast values by using the first initialization technique, the procedure is as under. The forecast value of 98 in the α = .2 column was obtained by taking 100 (the preceding forecast) and adding to that

(.2) × (90-100). This generates the forecasted value of 98 which can then be used as the forecast for period 3. The process is repeated to get all the other forecast values under this column and also other columns with given .5 and .9 values for α. The observed values and the forecast values have also been shown in Figure 3.2.

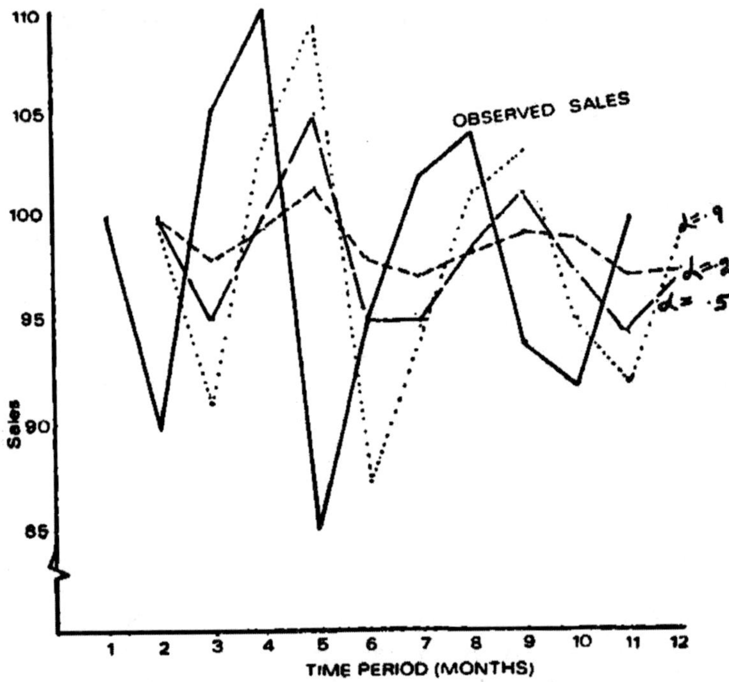

Fig. 3.2: Sales of 'X' Actual and Exponential Smoothing Forecasts

The impact of the alpha values on the forecast values is discernible from Table 3.4 as well as from the graph in Figure-3.2. A glance at these would show that the value of α (.9) gives very little smoothing in the forecast, whereas a small value of α (.2) gives reasonable smoothing. Then it may be concluded that smaller a value makes much better forecast than the larger values of α.

It is evident from the foregoing analysis that the single exponential smoothing wins some points over the moving average techniques. To repeat, single exponential smoothing requires little storage and a few computations. Forecasting with this technique can be generated by the use of very simple formula and limited data thus saving time and money. This is why exponentially weighted averages have replaced moving averages as the predominant technique used in short-term forecasting. This technique now finds extensive application in a number of business and economic situations. This is, among other factors, as reported, due to its simplicity, straightforwardness and appealing nature.

But the major problem associated with this and which also inhibits its wider application is to determine the optimal value for a which reflects the actual importance of historical data on future forecasts. The value is chosen through trial and error technique. The a value which will give the minimum mean square error is preferably chosen. The following rule of thumb, however, may be of some help in determining the value of alpha. The rule is: when there exists more randomness in the series, it is desirable to select small value of alpha and vice-versa.

Higher Forms of Smoothing

Like double moving average, there is double exponential smoothing (Brown's one Parameter Linear technique and Holt's two Parameter technique) and also triple exponential smoothing (Brown's one Parameter Quadratic technique and Winters' Three Parameter Trend and Seasonality technique) and also Pegels' technique of exponential smoothing. It is beyond the scope of this book to attempt all these. Our intent here had been simply to highlight the working and utility of the technique and not to attempt all exponential procedures.

To round up the discussion of the major smoothing techniques, it may be said that these techniques are widely used on account of their simplicity and low cost. These techniques are particularly useful when forecasts are required for many items, as is the case in many inventory systems. But it is to be admitted that better forecasting results are possible to obtain with more sophisticated techniques that can handle more complex patterns of data.

3.3. Decomposition Techniques

In the forecasting techniques discussed so far, it was not attempted to break a time series into its major sub-components viz., cycle, seasonality and randomness. Now a stage has been reached where an attempt will be made to analyze each component of the time series separately and then to develop a final forecast. This technique of decomposition forecasting has found wide acceptance because of its intuitive and straight forwardness appeal. Tracing the history of these techniques, it would be revealed that these techniques originated duriog the beginning of this century and are among the oldest forecasting techniques. The process of decomposition was first introduced by Macauley who developed ratio-to-moving averages technique in the 1920s. Since then this approach has bsen used widely and got further impetus with the introduction and widespread use of computers. There are several alternative approaches to decomposing a time series. The techniques of simple averages and ratio-to-trend, used in the past, have now lost much of their appeal in favour of ratio-to-moving averages.

As said above, many time series possess all the four components. A time series that appears to contain a smoothly increasing (or decreasing) component is said to contain a trend term. Although most trends are upward but this is not always necessarily to be so. The cyclical factors in time series generally reveal rhythmic variations in the economic series and follow the pattern of wave fluctuating from a high to a low value and back to the high value. Seasonal variations, or variations caused by weather patterns and or social habits produce an annual pattern in the time series. Irregular or random component which is the fourth component does also persist in the time series. This may be due to factors like wars, strikes, natural catastrophies or any other like factors which cannot be foreseen or controlled properly. These four components can well be represented mathematically in terms of decomposition approach as under :

$$X_t = f(I_{t,} C_{t,} R_t),$$

where X_t is the time series value (actual data) at period *t*.

I_t is the seasonal index at period *t,*

T_t is the trend component at period *t,*

C_t is the cyclical component at period t, and

R_t is the randomness component at period *t.*

It is to be remembered that these components vary in their importance and strength depending on the situation. It is very important for the purpose of forecasting to study and identify the past sub-patterns of each of the components in the series. For instance, in the very short run, the trend and cycle components may have changed very little, so forecasts of seasonal component are the most important. Similarly, in long term forecasting, the trend is usually dominant and the other two components are of relatively minor importance. In the medium period, all the components could be equally important and thus should be considered accordingly.

It is to be emphasized here again that decomposition can assume an additive or multiplicative model and can be of varying forms. For example, the decomposition technique of simple averages assumes the additive model of the following type.

$$X_t = (I_t + T_t + C_t + R_t)$$

The ratio-to-trend technique and ratio-to-moving averages use a multiplicative model of the form :

$$X_t = (I_t \times T_t \times C_t \times R_t).$$

3.3.1 *Ratio-to-moving Averages*: Let us now take a very simple example to show how forecasting is done with decomposition technique. We choose here ratio-to-moving average technique for the purpose of illustration. In Table 3.5, 5 years of (1983-1987) quarterly sales of product *'X'* is given which is assumed to have some trend, seasonally and other types of fluctuations. We want to forecast sales of *'X'* product for the 1st quarter of 1988.

Table 3.5: Quarterly Data for Product 'X' (1983-1987)

Period	*Quarters*			
	I	*II*	*III*	*IV*
1983	50	55	45	48
1984	52	57	50	52
1985	55	60	52	54
1986	60	65	62	63
1987	70	76	70	72

In order to prepare forecast, we are to identify *T, C, I* and *R* by analyzing the original data X

To forecast future values by applying decomposition involves certain steps as under:

STEP-I—ISOLATION OF SEASONALITY AND RANDOMNESS. To take an average of four quarters of the year 1983

This gives:

$$50 + 55 + 45 + 48 = \frac{198}{4} = 49.50$$

This figure 49.50 is the average for the year as a whole, and obviously excludes seasonality. This figure has also no randomness, since randomness fluctuates around zero. By adding these four values of the quarters, randomness tends to cancel itself since both positive and negative fluctuations are combined. If the values from the second quarter of the year 1983 to the value of the first quarter of the next year 1984 are added then the average works out to be

$$55 + 45 + 48 + 52 = \frac{200}{4} = 50.00$$

It again is the mean of four quarters which does not include seasonally and also no randomness but only trend and cycle. This moving process is to be repeated from the beginning to the end of the series. And the resultant moving averages including only trend and cycle $(T \times C)$ are shown in the following Table

Table 3.6: Product 'X' Moving Averages $T \times C$

Period	*Quarters*			
	I	*II*	*III*	*IV*
1983	—	—	49.50	50.00
1984	50.50	51.75	52.75	53.50
1985	54.25	54.75	55.25	56.50
1986	57.75	60.25	62.50	65.00
1987	67.75	69.75	72.00	—

Table 3.6 above shows the moving averages for the data of Table 3.5. And these moving averages include no seasonality and a minimum amount of randomness. They include only trend and cycle and can be written as

Moving Averages (MA) = T × C

For obtaining only the seasonality and randomness the actual values are to be divided by the moving averages which will give $I \times R$ Ratio. These valus are given in larger Table 3.7 and also in Table 3.8.

$$\frac{\text{ActualValues (X)}}{\text{Moving Average (M A)}} = \frac{T \times C \times I \times R}{T \times C} = I \times R$$

In order to find only seasonality, randomness is to be eliminated. As we know, randomness refers to chance and its value fluctuates around zero And if several random values are added, this will give a zero value or very close to zero. Randomness is eliminated by taking average of all I, II, III and IV quarters of all the years and these represent only seasonally, as random values when summed will result in zero or close to zero :

Table 3.7: Product 'X' — Moving Averages

Year	*Quarter*	*Data*	*T × C Moving Average*	*I × R Ratio*
1983	1	50	—	—
	2	55	—	—
	3	45	49.50	90.91
	4	48	50.00	96.00
1984	5	52	50.50	102.97
	6	57	51.75	110.14
	7	50	52.75	94.79
	8	52	53.50	97.20
1985	9	55	54.25	101.38
	10	60	54.75	109.59
	11	52	55.25	94.12
	12	54	56.50	95.58
1986	13	60	57.75	103.90
	14	65	60.25	107.88
	15	62	62.50	99.20
	16	63	65.00	96.92
1987	17	70	67.75	103.32
	18	76	69.75	108.96
	19	70	72.00	97.22
	20	72	—	—

Table 3.8: Product 'X' — Seasonality

	Quarters				
Period	*1st*	*IInd*	*IIIrd*	*IVth*	
1983	—	—	90.91	96.00	
1984	102.97	110.14	94.79	97.20	
1985	101.38	109.59	94.12	95.58	
1986	103.90	107.88	99.20	96.92	
1987	103.32	108.96	97.22	—	
	Mean or Average of Quarters				
	1st	*IInd*	*IIIrd*	*IVth*	*Total*
I	102.89 +	109.14 +	95.25 +	96.43 =	403.71
I (.9908)	101.94 +	108.14 +	94.37 +	95.55 =	400

$$\frac{400}{403.71} = .9908$$

It is seen from Table 3.8 that adding the four seasonal factors do not give a value of 400 and a simple adjustment is needed to obtain the average value of 100. This is done by dividing 400 by the sum 403.71 which will give .9908. If this is multiplied with each of the seasonal factors then it will give values 101.94, 108.14, 94.37 and 95.55 and their sum would now be exactly 400. This will help in understanding the seasonal factor more clearly. For example, the seasonal factor of 101.94 implies that the first quarter is 1.94 per cent higher than the average for the year and so on. In fact, the ratio values which vary around 100, give the effects of seasonality on the average deseasonalised values.

STEP-11—SEPARATING THE CYCLE FROM THE TREND: This is the second and the final step in the decomposition of time series. In order to separate the cycle from the trend it is necessary to identify the type of trend that appropriately describes the data. The trend may be of several forms like linear, exponential, S-Curve or some other form. Form the data in Table 3-5 a linear trend appears to describe the trend. Our data sufficiently indicates a linear trend, and parameters a and b in the formula $y = a + bX$ describing linear trend are to be estimated. The dependent variable in this case is product 'X' values and the independent variable is time (t) i.e. 1, 2, 3, 4. The values of a and b by applying the formula are:

$$a = 44.9$$

$$b = 1.29$$

The trend for each quarter is

$$T_t = a + b_t = 44.9 + 1.29\ (t)$$

For quarter 8, i.e., the fourth quarter of 1984 the linear trend value is:

$$T_3 = 44\ 9 + 1.29\ (8) = 55.22$$

Similarly, the values of all other quarters can be obtained. The cycle values (C) can be obtained as under

$$\frac{MA}{T} = \frac{T \times C}{T} = C$$

Therefore, the cycle of period 8 can be obtained by dividing the moving average from Table (detailed Table 3.7) by the corresponding trend value and then multiplying it by 100.

$$C_8 = \frac{53.50}{55.22} \times 100 = 96.89$$

Similarly, cycle values for all other quarters can be obtained. These values fluctuate around 100 giving thereby cyclical factors higher than average (greater than 100) or lower than average (less than 100).

We have isolated above all the components of time series by applying decomposition technique. Now, it is possible to develop a forecast based on the seasonal index, the trend and the cyclical factors which have been adequately identified. In order to illustrate, let us prepare a forecast for the first quarter of 1988. For this, the trend value for the period to be forecast is multiplied by the suitable seasonal index and by the suitable cyclical factor. Let us assume the value of cyclical[1] factor to be 99, then the forecast for this quarter would be

$S_{21} = [a + b\,(21)]$ (seasonal index first quarter) (cycle factor)

$$S_{21} = \left[44.9 + 1.29\,(21)\right]\left(\frac{101.94}{100}\right)\left(\frac{99}{100}\right) = 72.65$$

In developing forecast, the trend value for the period to be forecast is multiplied by the appropriate seasonal index and by the appropriate cyclical factor. Here we may recall the basic relationship

$$S = I \times T \times C \times R$$

In developing forecast last term cannot be determined so the relationships for forecasting simply would be

$$S_F = I \times T \times C$$

---

1. Cyclical factor (C) is wholly estimated on the basis of judgement- Estimating the cyclical factor may not be a straightforward task. This requires at least some knowledge of the level of economic activity during the period under forecast.

Similarly, the forecasts for other quarters of future years can be computed.

This technique of forecasting is quite attractive to the management due to its simplicity. The basic limitation of the technique, however, is that sometimes the various sub-patterns of the time series cannot be separated very clearly. And because of this factor, there is growing preference for the application of regression technique over the decomposition technique of forecasting.

Chapter Four

Quantitative Forecasting Techniques-II (Explanatory and Other Techniques)

In this chapter, explanatory and some other quantitative forecasting techniques, which have not been discussed in the preceding chapter, are discussed. The techniques included are: Regression Model of Forecasting, Econometric Model, Input-Output Model, the Box-Jenkins Technique, Barometric Forecasting Technique, and Cycle Forecasting. The first three techniques namely the Regression Model, Econometric Model and Input-Output Model may be termed as Explanatory Forecasting Techniques. An explanatory model is one that presents an equation explaining the value of the variable of interest in terms of present values of one or more other variables, and possibly also the past values of these variables.

4.1 Regression Model of Forecasting

With regression analysis, we can attempt to develop forecasting. The formulation and estimation of regression relationships is a major topic in classical statistics and a complete account can be found in any statistics text. The usual forecasting procedure using a regression model is to deal with one dependent measure say sales and one independent measure say advertising. This is, as pointed out, is an explanatory model, and an equation explaining this relationship between dependent and independent variables can be determined. Regression may be simple and multiple. In a simple regression there are only two variables. Multiple regression involves more than two variables. We consider now these two types of regression techniques in relation to forecasting.

4.1.1. *Simple Regression*: In simple regression only two variables are considered and assuming a straight-line relationship (linear relationship), the mathematical function can take the following form:

$$y = a + bx$$

where y is dependent variable

a is intercept, i.e., the value of y where $x = 0$

b is regression coefficient and indicates how much the value of y changes when value of x changes by one unit. It is also the slope of the regression line, and a and b are two parameters in the equation for a straight line.

It is pertinent to mention that non-linear functions can also be transformed into linear[1] by suitable techniques (it is beyond the scope of this text), and then applying simple regression analysis with its assumptions of linear relationship to many situations successfully. Regression is much superior tool of forecasting over purely time series techniques in that it can be used for causal as well as with time-series models. It also gives more precise results as it uses a statistical model. This model of forecasting can be used by computing the values of a and b the two unknown in the regression equation. There are several techniques available for computing the values of these two unknown. The technique of 'least square', however, gives the best result and is generally applied. This is

1. Regression may be linear, which means a relationship that can be represented graphically by a straight line. If the relationship is represented on a graph and forms a curve, it is called curvilinear regression.

a technique of fitting a straight line to historical observations. The logic for using this technique of 'least square' is that the distance between the actual observations and corresponding points on the regression line is minimized. Alternatively stated, by doing so the sum of the squared deviations (errors) is made as small as possible in choosing *a* and *b*. Mathematically $\Sigma(yi - y_{ie})^2$ is minimized and also the summation of the deviations equals zero. Here y_4 are the observed values and y_{ie} the estimated values of *y* by the regression line and these, in fact, are the forecasted values.

In order to turn the above argument in practice, let us take an example and see how the relevant computations are made for achieving a forecast figure, *i.e.*, how regression model can be used to forecast *y* values with given corresponding *x* values. The example purposely is kept simple.

Example: Obtain the forecast sales for period 21 from the data in Table 4.1.

Table 4.1: Sales of 'Y'

X (Period)	1	2	3	4	5	6	7	8	9	10	
Y (Actual)	50	55	45	48	52	57	50	52	55	60	
X (Period)	11	12	13	14	15	16	17	18	19	20	21
Y (Actual)	52	54	60	65	62	63	70	76	70	72	—

The necessary calculations are shown in Table 4.2. Following the calculations, the sales forecast for any period can be made. The sales forecast for period 21 would be

$$yc = 44.90 + 1.29\ (21) = 71.99$$

Similarly, sales forecast for all other periods after 21 can be made by using the above values and indicating the period.

$$\bar{x} = \frac{\Sigma x}{N} = \frac{210}{20} = 10.5 \quad \bar{y} = \frac{\Sigma y}{N} = \frac{1168}{20} = 58.4$$

$$\sigma x = \sqrt{\frac{\Sigma dx^2}{N}} = \sqrt{\frac{665}{20}} = 5.77$$

$$\sigma y = \sqrt{\frac{\Sigma dy^2}{N}} = \sqrt{\frac{1442}{20}} = 8.49$$

$$r = \frac{\Sigma dx \times dy}{N\sigma x \times \sigma y} = \frac{862.00}{20 \times 5.77 \times 8.49} = \frac{862.00}{979.7} = +.88$$

Table 4.2: Computing Regression

Period X	Actual Sales y (Units)	dx $(x - \bar{x})$	dx^2	dy $(y - \bar{y})$	dy^2	dx × dy	Estimated Sales ye
1.	50	–9.5	90.25	–8.4	70.56	79,80	46.19
2.	55	–8.5	72.25	–3.4	11.56	28.90	47.48
3.	45	–7.5	56.25	–13.4	179.56	100.50	48.77
4.	48	–6.5	42.25	–10.4	108.16	67.60	50.06
5.	52	–5.5	30.25	–6.4	40.96	35.20	51.35
6.	57	–4.5	20.25	–1.4	1.96	6.30	52.64
7.	50	–3.5	12.25	–8.4	70.56	29.40	53.93
8.	52	–2.5	6.25	–6.4	40.96	16.00	55.22
9.	55	–1.5	2.25	–3.4	11.56	5.10	56.51
10.	60	–.5	.25	1.6	2.56	–.80	57.80
11.	52	.5	.25	–6.4	40.96	–3.20	59.09
12.	54	1.5	2.25	–4.4	19.36	–6.60	60.38
13.	60	2.5	6.25	1.6	2.56	4.00	61.67
14.	65	3.5	12.25	6.6	43.56	23.10	62.96
15.	62	4.5	20.25	3.6	12.96	16.20	64.25
16.	63	5.5	30.25	4.6	21.16	25.30	65.54
17.	70	6.5	42.25	11.6	134.56	75.40	66.83
18.	76	7.5	56.25	17.6	309.76	132.00	68.12
19.	70	8.5	72.25	11.6	134.56	98.60	69.41
20.	72	9.5	90.25	13.6	184.96	129.20	70.70
21.	–	–	–	–	–	–	71.99
Σ=210	1168		665.00		1442.80	862.00	

Regression Equation *y* on *x*

$$\left(y-\bar{y}\right)=r\frac{\sigma y}{\sigma x}(x-\bar{x})$$

$$y-58.4=.88\frac{8.49}{5.77}(x-10.5)$$

y - 58.4 = .88 X 1.471 $(x$ - 10.5)

$y - 58.4 = 1.29\ (x - 10.5)$

$y - 58.4 = 1.29\ x - 13.5$

$y = 1.29\ x - 13.5 + 58.4$

$y = 1.29\ \text{x} + 44.90$

$y = \text{a} + b\ x$

$y = 44.90 + 1.29\ x$

y when x is $1 = 44.90 + 1.29 \times 1 = 46.19$

y when x is $21 = 44.90 + 1.29 \times 21 = 71.99$

The final results of the computation can also be shown in Figure 4.1. A logical approach to forecast future values would be to fit a straight line to the data as to obtain a reasonable spread of observations either side of the line and then to extrapolate (i.e. extend) that line to produce forecasts.

In Figure 4.1 each dotted point represents the sales volume(y) in a given year. The regression equation $y = a + b\ (x_i)$ describes the variation in the values of y for the given changes in x and is used for estimating the value of y for the given value of x. Notice that in the regression line, a is the intercept of the regression line with the sales axis, b is the slope of the line, a is the distance between the point of origin and the point where regression line touches y axis. The regression line is determined by the values of a and b, and presents the best fitting or least squares line. It is obvious that a straight line has been drawn on the basis of equation that best represents the relationship inherent in the data points of the scatter diagram. It is also clear that in most cases the actual values of y differ from our calculated ye values. And the line minimizes the sum of the squared vertical distances between each point on the scatter diagram and the line. The line is generally called an ordinary least square or regression line. And by extending the line, the value of independent variable can be inserted into the regression function and can be estimated. For instance, the forecast sale values in the period 21 would be 71.99 units and which is on the extended straight line.

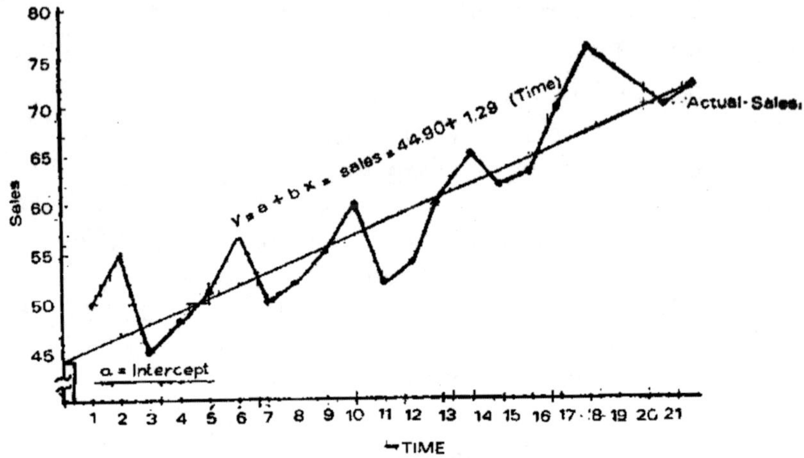

Fig. 4.1 Actual Sales and Regression Line Relating Sales to Time

The technique of linear regression which essentially fits a straight line to a series of observed values, is a good and well defined powerful statistical tool. The development of computer has established regression technique as a major forecasting technique. However, it must be kept in mind that:

(i) This technique requires more data than exponential smoothing models to produce sensible forecasts.

(ii) This cannot be updated, other than by performing a further complete analysis when more data become available.

(iii) This is totally inappropriate for generating seasonal forecasting.

Despite these limitations, it is very useful forecasting technique. In fact, with this technique of forecasting lone can move from intuitive evaluation of the relationships among variables to precise quantified knowledge. In many situations, this is very potent and suitable technique of forecasting. As we shall see further in this chapter, it has become a standard tool with the econometricians in pursuance of their research.

4.1.2 *Multiple Regression.* The multiple regression technique of forecasting is just the extension of simple regression forecasting technique. In multiple regression there are two or more independent variables and one dependent variable which is to be predicted. The relation between these variables would be expressed in terms of the following equations.

$$y_e = a + b_1x_1 + b_2x_2 + \ldots + b_nX_n$$

Where y_e = Estimated Sales

X_1 = time

x_2 = advertising

x_n = Several other factors such as prices, competition, budget etc.

For the sake of simplicity, let us consider only two variables x_1 and x_2 which have considerable influence on the level of sales (y). If it is so then sales can be predicted with any given value of x_1 and x_2. We are to find out first, as in simple regression, the values of a, b_1 and b_2 by the technique of least squares.

To illustrate the application of multiple regression in forecasting, we take the following example:

Table 4.3: Sales, Advertisement and Price

Year	*Sales* y	*Advertisement* x_1	*Price* x_2
1981	40	10	36
1982	45	20	33
1983	50	*30*	37
1984	65	40	37
1985	70	50	34
1986	70	*60*	32
1987	80	70	36
1988	—	—	—

The task is to prepare a forecast, on the basis of information for the company's sales, for the year 1988. The computations are given in Table 4.4.

$$\bar{X}_1 = \frac{\Sigma X_1}{N} = \frac{280}{7} = 40, \bar{X}_2 = \frac{\Sigma X_2}{N} = \frac{245}{7} = 35,$$

$$\bar{Y} = \frac{\Sigma Y}{N} = \frac{420}{7} = 60$$

$$\left.\begin{aligned} \Sigma x_1 y &= b_1 \Sigma x_1^2 + b_2 \Sigma x_1 x_2 \\ \Sigma x_2 y &= b_1 \Sigma x_1 x_2 + b_2 \Sigma x_2^2 \end{aligned}\right] \begin{aligned} 1900 &= 2800\, b_1 - 50\, b_2 \quad \text{(i)} \\ -20 &= -50\, b_1 + 24\, b_2 \quad \text{(ii)} \end{aligned}$$

$$1900 = 2800\, b_1 - 50\, b_2 \qquad \text{(i)}$$

$$(+) - 1120 = -2800\, b_1 + 1344\, b_2 \qquad \text{(ii)} \times 56$$

$$780 = + 1294\, b_2$$

$$\text{or} \quad .603 = b_2$$

By substituting the Value of b_2 in equation (ii) :

$$-20 = -50\, b_1 + 24\, (.603)$$

$$\text{or} \quad -20 = -50\, b_1 + 14.472 \text{ or } 50\, b_1 = 14.472 + 20 = 34.472$$

$$\text{or } b_1 = .689$$

$$a = \bar{y} - b_1 \bar{x}_1 - b_2 \bar{x}_2, \qquad \text{or } a = 60 - .689\,(40) - .603\,(35)$$

$$\text{or } a = 60 - 27.560 - 21.105$$

$$= 11.335$$

The regression equation will be $y_e = a + b_1x_1 + b_2x_2$

$$\text{or } y_e = 11.335 + .689x_1 + .603\, x_2$$

The value of y_e when $x_1 = 80$ and $x_2 = 37$ (these are assumed values)

$$y_e = 11.335 + .689\,(80) + .603\,(37)$$

$$y_e = 11.335 + 55.120 + 22.311$$

$$y_e = 88.766$$

Table 4.4: Computing Regression

Year	Adv. x_1	Price x_2	Sales y	$(x_1-\bar{x}_1)$ x_1	$(x_2-\bar{x}_2)$ x_2	$y-\hat{y}$ y	x_1y	x_1^2	x_1x_2	x_2y	x_2^2
1981	10	36	40	−30	+1	−20	600	900	−30	−20	1
1982	20	33	45	−20	−2	−15	300	400	+40	+30	4
1983	30	37	50	−10	+2	−10	100	100	−20	−20	4
1984	40	37	65	0	+2	+5	0	0	0	+10	4
1985	50	34	70	+10	−1	+10	100	100	−10	−10	1
1986	60	32	70	+20	−3	+10	200	400	−60	−30	9
1987	70	36	80	+30	+1	+20	600	900	+30	+20	1
Σ =	280	245	420				1900	2800	−50	−20	24

The forecast sales volume in the year 1988 would be 88.77 units provided the values regarding advertising and price are true. The forecast sales for other years can also be obtained by assigning the appropriate values for x_1 and x_2 into the multiple regression equation. Since the forecast is to be prepared on the basis of the independent variables, so these should be estimated correctly and properly otherwise there would remain error in forecasting.

The technique of multiple regression is based on certain assumptions which should be thoroughly checked and understood before applying this technique.

The first assumption inherent in the application of the technique of least squares is that of linearity which means that the dependent variable is linearly related to each of the independent variables. Thus, the technique should be used only when this condition is satisfied. The second assumption is that the variance and the amount of variations do not change over the range of observation, i.e., variations remain constant over the range. Third assumption is that of residual being normally distributed. This is not a very restrictive assumption particularly when observations exceed 30.

Besides these assumptions, the basic limitation of the application of multiple regression is that of multicollinearity. It is a computational problem that arises when two or more of the independent variables are highly correlated. Thus it should be seen that independent vaiables selected are highly correlated with y but are not correlated with one another. This is very often the case in economic and business problems. Finally, it should be said that while using regression equation for forecasting purpose, r^2 (coefficient of determination) must be worked out. If it gives high value, say .90, then the manager can use the regression equation with great confidence as this explaines 90 per cent of the total variation—, i.e., the variations in x_1 and x_2 explain 90 per cent of the variations in the sales.

Largely because of the cost factor, as the new set of data is to be drawn when the causal relationship between the independent variables and the dependent variables changes (which is true in the dynamic world), the technique is generally used for medium and larger terms forecasting. It can be concluded that regression model can be very useful in the hands of a creative and imaginative forecaster who should use it with utmost precautions.

4.1.3 *Regression Statistics* : There is available what is called regression statistics that can be used to infer the strength of the concept. These statistics are described below.

COEFFICIENT OF DETERMINATION: The coefficient of determination[1] is typically indicated by the symbol r^2. This measures the strength of association between y and x. It is simply equal to the ratio of variation in y that is explained by the regression equation to the total variation in y.

$$r^2 = \frac{\text{Explained Variation}}{\text{Total Variation}}$$

r^2 can take values ranging from 0, indicating that the model absolutely provides no explanation of variation in the dependent variable, to 1.0, indicating that all the variation has been explained by the independent variables.

Total variation of y is, by definition, the sum of the squared deviations about the mean value of y, that is

$$\text{Total Variation in } y = \sum_{t=1}^{n} (y_t - \bar{y})^2$$

1. We send to use r^2 in case of coefficient of multiple determination. Although the calculation of the coefficient of multiple determination is more complex thant he simply coefficient of determination. The concept is analogous and the interpretation is the same. That is, they are both equal to the ratio of the explained variation to the total variation of y.

The deviations of each observed value, y_t, from the mean value, $\bar{y}$ are squared, then these squares are summed to arrive at the total variation in y. If y were a constant, y_t would equal $\bar{y}$ for all observations, and there would be no variance in y.

It is to be seen that the total variation of y can be partitioned into two parts: (i) the variation explained by changes in the independent variables, and (ii) the variation that cannot be explained by the regression model.

$$\text{Explained variation} = \sum_{t=1}^{n} = (\hat{y}_t - \bar{y})^2$$

$$\text{Unexplained variation} = \sum_{t=1}^{n} = (y_t - \hat{y})^2$$

If all the data points lay exactly on the regression line, that is, if $y_t = \hat{y}_t$ for all values of t—there would be no unexplained variation. The total variation must be equal to the sum of the unexplained and explained variations, so one can write

$$\Sigma(y_t - \bar{y})^2 = \Sigma(\hat{y}_t - \bar{y}) + \Sigma(y_t - \bar{y}_t)^2$$

The coefficient of determination is then calculated as follows:

$$r^2 = \frac{\Sigma(\hat{y}_t - \bar{y})^2}{\Sigma(y_t - \bar{y})^2}$$

For our example, the problem of Table 4.1, the coefficient of determination is .774.

An r^2 of .774 indicates that 77 per cent of variation in the dependent variable has been explained by the independent variable. If r^2 is 1 then each data point for the dependent period must exactly be on the regression line. Obviously, as the size of the deviations about the regression curve increases, the coefficient of determination will fall. If r^2 is zero then in such a case the regression equation fails to explain totally any variation in the dependent variable. For our example, where the value of r^2 is .774, indicates that about 77 percent of variation in sales has been explained by time, and is quite acceptable.

To conclude, we may say that when the coefficient of determination is very low, it is an indication that the model is inadequate for explaining the sales in terms of time. This will suggest then that there are some other important variables which have been omitted to explain the model and the fit of the regression line is a poor one.

STANDARD ERROR OF THE ESTIMATE : This is another statistics which helps in determining the accuracy of the regression model. With this we can determine a range within which prediction of the dependent variable can be done with varying degrees of statistical confidence. This measures the variation around the line of the best fit. This measure is the standard deviation of the errors of estimating y for x or x for y. If the actual and estimated values are the same, the standard error of the estimate will be zero. In such a case correlation must be perfect and all estimates made from the regression equation must be perfect. The formula for computing standard error of the estimate is

$$S_{yx} = \frac{\Sigma(y - \bar{y})^2}{n - k}$$

where

S_{yx} = Standard error of estimate for y on x

$y - \bar{y}$ = deviation between actual and computed value of y variable.

n = Number of items

k = Number of constants in the regression equation.

The standard error of the estimate can indicate the precision with which the regression model can be expected to predict the dependent variable. This will estimate to determine just how accurate a prediction $\hat{y}_t$ is likely to be. It is to be mentioned that greater prediction accuracy is associated with smaller standard errors of the estimate.

MULTICOLLINEARITY: The problem of multicollinearity may exist in regression analysis. This problem can be troublesome in multiple regression analysis. Multicollinearity occurs when two or more of the independent variables are so highly correlated that it becomes very difficult to separate them and to measure their relative effects very precisely. The existence of this situation would violate the assumption concerning multiple regression. This assumption is that there is no strong linear relationship among the independent variables. If independent variables have high correlated values then 'independent' variables are not really independent of one another. In order to avoid this problem of multicollinearity a constant check should be made of the correlation coefficient and drop one or more of the highly correlated variables from the regression. But in case of forecasting, it is not necessary to do it, that is, to exclude either of the independent variables that are highly correlated. In fact, the predictive power will probably be better with both variables included in.the regression.

4.2 Econometric Model of Forecasting

Econometric model is another explanatory technique which is available to the managers for forecasting. Econometrics is defined as the application of statistical and mathematical tools for the purpose of testing the validity or reasonableness of economic hypothesis. Econometric is mainly concerned with macro economic models. It was not until the late 1960s that the econometric model approach was used for forecasting purposes. Since then there have been many efforts to construct econometric models for developing forecasts. Econometric model is a system of linear equations involving several interdependent variables. There are, in broader sense, two types of variables viz., endogenous and exogenous. Variables that are determined within the model are called endogenous variables, while those that are inputs into the model—such variables as reflecting fiscal and monetary policy, are referred to as exogenous variables.

It is to be noted that regression and econometric models have many things in common but also at the same time possess different characteristics. While making distinction between a regression model and an econometric model, it may be said that simple regression is a special case of multiple regression, while the latter being a special case of an econometric model. Multiple regression involves a single equation, whereas an econometric model can include any number of simultaneous multiple regression, equations. Actually, the basic premise of econometric modeling is that everything in the real world depends upon everything else. Econometric model enables the forecaster to take into account the simultaneous interaction between dependent and independent variables, while it is not possible in case of regression model.

4.2.1 *Estimation Procedure.* As indicated, an econometric model would consider various variables simultaneously. Thus, the task of specifying right kind and number of these variables required in the model is quite formidable. Broadly speaking, there are the following two types of estimation procedures:

(i) Single Equation Estimation

(ii) Multiple Equation Estimation

(i) SINGLE EQUATION ESTIMATION. This approach is straightforward and is the simplest form of econometric model of forecasting. The econometrician would first develop hypothesis concerning the relationships between a set of variables and a certain economic phenomenon. And then by making use of his knowledge of economic theory and mathematical model building, the econometrician would formulate his hypothesis which he expresses in a precise functional relationship form. For example, in constructing a model for the sales of say

Maruti car, one might hypothesize that car demand *(Q)* is determined by price *(P)*, disposable income *(Yd)*, population *(Pop)*, personal liquidity (L), availability of credit (C), and advertising expenditures *(A)*. A linear model assuming that the relationships are linear, could be written as under:

$$Q = a_0 + a_1 P + a_2 Yd + a_3 Pop + a_4 L + a_5 C + a_6 A$$

Once the economic relationship has been expressed in equation form, the next task is to estimate the parameters of the system, or values of the a's in equation above. These values can be estimated by the technique of least square regression analysis.

Once the parameters or coefficients of the model have been obtained, the forecaster would estimate for the future values of the independent variables in the model. Substituting these values into the model, a forecast value for the dependent variable is developed, i.e., the demand for car can be estimated. It is clear that in single equation model the future values of the independent variables must be easily obtainable.

Single equation model may serve the purpose of forecasting, and business problems can be analyzed with its use. But in many cases, the inter-relationships involved are so complex that may not be tackled adequately with single equation system. Under such situation, the use of multiple equation system becomes absolutely necessary.

(ii) Multiple Equation System. In this system of multiple equation, numerous variables that affect the phenomenon endogenously or exogenously are included. The variables within the model are referred to as endogenous variables, while the other variables in the model, future values of which must be provided from some external source, are called exogenous variables and may include such things as the level of government expenditure or the level of exports.

An econometric model (multiple), in fact, has two kinds of equations, identities and behavioural equations.

Identities or definitional equations express relationships that are true by definition. For instance, profit (P) is equal to Total Revenue (TR) minus Total Cost (TC) is an identity.

$$P = TR - TC$$

The second type of equation, behavioural or structural equation explains the relationship between a particular endogenous variable and other variables in the system. Since each endogenous variable must be explained by one structural equation, it becomes necessary that the number of structural equations in the model be exactly equal to the number of endogenous variables.

Let us take a very simple example to illustrate it. Perhaps the easiest way to illustrate the use of multiple equation system is to examine a simple three equation model of a national economy. No doubt, in practice econometric models are often rather complex and also quite large. We have selected only three equations model as to give insight into the technique without confusion. The three equations are as under:

$$Ct = a_1 + b_1 \text{ GNPt} + V_1, \qquad \text{(i)}$$

$$I_t = a_2 + b_2 \, Pt\text{-}i + V_2, \qquad \text{(ii)}$$

$$\text{GNP}_t = C_t + I_t + G_t. \qquad \text{(iii)}$$

Where

C = Personal Consumption Expenditure

I = Net Capital Investment

P = Profits

G = Government Expenditures for Goods and Services

GNP = Gross National Product

a, b = Parameters of the Equations

v = Stochastic Disturbance Terms

t = Current Time Period

$t\text{-}_1$ = Previous Time Period

Equations (i) and (ii) are behavioural or structural equations. Equation (iii) is an identity or definitional. It defines gross national product as being equal to the consumption expenditures, net capital investment and government expenditures. V in equations (i) and (ii) reflect the fact that the theoretical relationships are not exact. But to the extent these stochastic elements are randomly distributed and their net effects are cancelled with an expected value of zero— they do not pose a threat to emprical estimation of parameters. Using either ordinary least squares or some simultaneous estimation procedure, we can arrive at estimates of a, a_1 and b_1 b_2. Solving the system of equations simultaneously and substituting equation (i) into (iii)—that is, replacing C_t with equation (i)—we get

$$GNP_t = a_1 + b_1 \, GNP_t + I_t + G_t \qquad \text{(iv)}$$

A similar substitution of equation (ii) for the variable I_t produces:

$$GNP_t = a_1 + b_1 \, GNP_t + a_2 + b_2 + P_{t-1} + G_t \qquad \text{(iv)}$$

Collecting terms and isolating GNP in equation (v) yields:

$$(1 - b_1) \, GNP_t = a_1 + a_2 + b_2 P_{t-1} + G_t,$$

or, alternatively:

$$GNP_t = \frac{a_1 + a_2 + b_2 P_{t-1} + G_t}{1 - b_1}$$

$$= \frac{a_1 + a_2}{1 - b_1} + \frac{b_2}{1 - b_1} P_{t-1} + \frac{1}{1 - b_1} G_t \qquad \text{(vi)}$$

Now the last equation (vi) relates current GNP to the previous period's profits and to current government expenditure. As a result, equation (vi) provides us with a forecasting model which leads us to the simultaneous relationship expressed in the multiple equation system.

4.2.2 *The Advantages and Limitations of Econometric Model*

ADVANTAGES

Forecasting models based on econometric methodology possess a number of significant advantages over the several other alternative types. The primary benefit of an econometric model is that it forces the forecaster to make explicit his assumptions about the inter-relationships between the variables in the economic system being examined. Alternatively stated, the forecaster must deal with causal relationship. This process would increase the reliability and acceptability of the results.

Another advantage of econometric models is that they predict not only the direction of change in an economic series but also the magnitude of the change.

A third advantage of these models lies in the consistency of the technique which remains from period to period. The forecaster is in a position to compare his forecasts with actual results and use the insights gained from this comparision to improve his model. The model can be modified, that is, existing parameters may be re-estimated and new variables or relationships developed, in order to improve future forecasts.

Finally, econometric models are invaluable tools for increasing the understanding of the way an economic system works and for testing and evaluating alternative policies of the organizations and the government.

LIMITATIONS

Econometric models, though sophisticated, are not without limitations. Some limitations are adduced as under :

First, a forecast made from an econometric model is not exact because the estimates of the model parameters are subject to sampling errors. The possibility that the theoretical relationships in the model may not be correct, cannot be ruled out completely.

Even, if they are valid, they are subject to change. So the models must be constructed with built-in-flexibility in order to facilitate the absorption of shifting relationship. In fact, the complexity in the specification and identification and in estimation of the variables make the econometrician's job a challenging one.

Second, the successful use of econometric model requires a great deal of skill, scientific knowledge and personal judgement.

Third, what should be correct size of the model, i. e., the number of equations that it should contain is also very controversial point. Some econometricians prefer a 'small' model of 20-30 structural equations, but models of 100 or more equations are considered necessary by other experts.

Fourth, the practical problem that has arisen in recent years is the use of non-linear forms of the variables in the structural equations. The usual practice is to "linearize" the model and then to try the solution. This practice may not be able to get optimal solution to the problem.

Fifth, this model cannot be used without a computer. Cost of using the model is tremendous. This has limited the application of econometric models in small and medium organizations. In practice, only the influential and affluent organizations make use of the model.

Sixth, there is absence of a set of rules that can be applied under all situations. This makes the development of econometric models highly dependent upon the specific situation and also requires the involvement of a skilled and experienced econometrician.

It may be said while concluding that the accuracy of these models depends heavily on the forecaster's skill in predicting the exogenous variables. These models are difficult and costly. Their usefulness in forecasting, which are generally aimed towards policy making, is also somewhat controversial.

4.3 Input-Output Forecasting

Input-output forecasting technique is considered to be the most sophisticated and promising technique. This approach provides the most complete examination of all the complex interrelationships within an economic system. Input-output forecasts are generated through the use of a device named Input-output tables developed by Professor Wassily Leontief.

An input-output table is a matrix with each row showing how the output or sales of a particular sector of the economy is distributed among all the sectors of the economy, including final demand. In the same fashion, each column indicates all the inputs used by a particular sector of the economy. Let us take very simple example to illustrate where an economy is classified into three industries, A, B and C. The input-output details for this type of economy are given in Table 4.5

Table 4.5: Input-output Matrix for a Hypothetical Economy
(Millions of Rs.)

		Purchasing Industries			*Final Demand*	*Total*
		A	*B*	*C*		
Selling Industries	A	10	50	20	100	180
	B	5	10	60	30	105
	C	70	5	—	45	120
Value added		95	40	40	—	175
Total		180	105	120	175	

It is clear from Table 4.5 that the output of any industry in the economy can either be purchased by the same industry or other producing industry in the economy or consumed as a final good by individuals, government and business. The "value added" row shows the resource cost for labour and capital incurred and the profit earned by the industry listed in column heading. It is obvious that row total for each industry equals the column total for the respective industry. It means that the sum of revenues for an industry identically equals the sum of costs incurred plus the profits earned.

For the forecasting purposes, we require three tables. The first is input-output matrix table or transactions table. This table permits systematic examinations of all the interrelationships among the various industries and final demand sectors. It indicates in each row how the output of goods and services of a given industry is distributed to all industries and final users in the economy. In our

Table 4.6: Direct Requirement Table for Input-output Analysis

		Purchasing Industries		
		A	*B*	*C*
Selling Industries	A	.056	.476	.167
	B	.028	.095	.500
	C	.389	.048	—
Value Added		.528	.381	.333

Table 4.7: Total Requirement Table for Input-output Analysis

		Purchasing Industries		
		A	*B*	*C*
Selling Industries	A	1.321	.726	.584
	B	.335	1.319	.716
	C	.530	.345	1.262

example, Industry *A* produces Rs. 180 of total output, of which Rs. 80 are intermediate goods sold to other industries (including Industry *A)* for use in producing other products, while the remaining Rs. 100 of output are finished goods that are sold to final consumers. Column 'A' shows the consumption of goods and services from all industries and the value added for a given industry.

Table 4.6, the direct requirement table, is derived from Table 4.5. The direct requirement figures in this Table are found by dividing each element in the industry columns in Table 4.5 by the column total. The shortcoming of the direct requirement table is that, as its name suggests, only direct requirements are shown and obviously does not take into account these "second round" effects of an increase in output in one industry.

Table 4.7 presents the total requirement—direct plus indirect— for the hypothetical economy. This table is also known as Leontief Inverse Matrix. This matrix is generated from the direct requiremeat table. Each column in the table shows the amount of total input, both direct and indirect, which each industry listed down the left side of the table must supply for the industry named in the column heading to produce one rupee of output for final demand. The computation of the values in the total requirements matrix is performed by solving for the elements of the $(I—A)^{-1}$ matrix, where I is an identity matrix and A is the $(n \times n)$ matrix of direct requirements. In our example n=3 since we have three interrelated industry sectors. This table is used along with econometric models in formulating industry forecasts.

In the present example, in order to determine the total output for each industry, the $(I—A)^{-1}$ matrix is to be multiplied by the final demand vector [which is an (n × 1) matrix].

Table 4.8: Total Requirement Matrix

			Final Demand Vector		*Total Demand Vector*
1.321	.726	.584	100		180
335	1.319	.716	30	=	105
530	.345	1.262	45		120

It may be noted that this product corresponds to the total demand or total output for industries *A, B* and C, respectively. From this we now can find (i) the total demand vector for any composite of industry final demand; and (ii) given the total demand for each industry's production, we can further compute the new transactions matrix; that is, how much Industry *B* will have to purchase from *A* and C, and how much *B* will use of their own output. The latter can be determined by multiplying each element in any column of the direct requirements matrix by the total demand for the corresponding industry. For instance, multiplying each element of column *A* in the direct requirement matrix by 180 would yield 10, 5, and 70, the elements of the transaction matrix in column A (180×.056), = 10, 180 × .028 = 5, and 180 × .389 = 70), This would mean that if industry *A* produces Rs 180 of total output then it will require Rs 5 of output from Industry *B*, Rs. 70 of output from industry *C* and Rs. 10 of its own product. In this way, forecast of total output (in revised total demand vector) for each industry can be obtained by varying the final demand for any one industry.

4.3.1 Advantages of the Model, One of the major advantages of input-output technique is that the forecast based on this is internally consistent, and would reveal, at once, the bottlenecks and supply problems in the economy.

Input-output models are used to generate final demand providing very detailed consumption forecasts. These forecasts of final demand are then "driven" through the total requirements table to obtain total industry forecasts.

The forecasts based on input-output tables are possible to make for regions, industries or even single business organization. In case of a single business organization, departments, or organizational units, these become the entries of the table among which the transactions can take place and for which forecasts can be made.

With the help of input-output analysis, the forecaster can easily specify and analyze the changes in technology by changing the direct requirement coefficients. This can be done by applying engineering estimates of technological change, fitting historical data of the coefficient conforming to some curve such as an *S*—shaped curve. This would also justify the assumption of constant coefficient, to a larger extent.

Lastly, it helps the businessmen to guide in their decision making process. For example, input-output has been used to evaluate markets prospects for established products, to identify potential market for new products, to spot prospective shortages in supplies, to add new dimensions and greater depth to the analysis of the economic environment in which the firms expect to operate. It also helps in evaluating investment prospects in various industries.

In summary, the major contribution of input-output analysis to the forecaster is that it facilitates a detailed training and measurement of the effects of all the demands both direct and indirect on the output of each industry influenced by an initial change in some final demand. In addition, forecasts that are generated by input-output analysis are internally consistent, making it possible for the forecaster to determine what effect changes in demand will have on various industries. The much greater details provided by these tables increase greatly their value to managerial decision makers. This should lead to much greater use of the tool of input output analysts for industry and firm forecasting purposes. Notably, input-output has now become a versatile tool for forecasting purposes.

4.4 The Box-Jenkins Forecasting Technique

This is a special type of forecasting technique proposed by George Box and Gwilym Jenkins in their book entitled *Time Series Analysis, Forecasting, and Control* in the year 1970. This technique to short-term forecasting has proved to be very useful. The Box-Jenkins technique of forecasting is particularly well suited to handle complex time series and other forecasting situations in which single data pattern exists instead a variety of data patterns. The real beauty of this technique lies in the fast that it can handle complex patterns with the help of relatively well specified set of rules. In the Box-Jenkins technique, there is no need to assume initially a fixed pattern. Rather the approach begins by assuming a tentative pattern that is fitted to the data so that the error is minimized. Not only this, it provides further clues for identifying the correct pattern of series.

The Box-Jenkins approach enables the forecaster to search for the relationship that best describes movements in the time series, by using only past monthly values of a particular time series. It is interesting to note that whereas regression and econometric techniques require the forecaster to specify the model, the Box-Jenkins approach simply begins with a tentative specification, as already indicated, and then is modified and corrected by applying a complicated search technique. This process would continue until the best specification for that time series is obtained.

It is to be remembered that the Box-Jenkins approach can be used only for the series that are stationary, that is, series that do not have a long term trend. Box-Jenkins' approach to forecasting is an integration of the autoregressive model with the moving average one to call it (ARIMA), i.e., Autoregressive/Integrated/Moving average. It is a mixture of Auto-regressive (AR) models introduced by Yule in 1926 and Moving Average (MA) models given by Slutzky in 1937. These two were combined by Wold in 1938 and gave a new name ARMA. However, the ARMA models were further extended by including seasonal time series and also the non-stationary processes and are called by the name (ARIMA) as given by Box-Jenkins. The Box Jenkins is the technique which aids in fitting an (ARMA) model to any set of data. According to Box-Jenkins approach, any stationary time series can be explained by one of the three models : (1) an autoregressive model; (2) a moving average model; and (3) an auto-regressive-moving average model.

Obviously, the objective of Box-Jenkins is to explain movements in the stationary series so that the error terms (e_t) are as small as can be, and are also uncorrelated with one another, that is, *et* is not correlated with previous period error terms.

The general term of autoregressive model is:

$$Y_t = a_1 Y_{t-1} + a_2 Y_{t-2} + a_3 Y_{t-3} + \ldots + a_n Y_{t-n} + e_t.$$

It is clear from the equation that the value of Y in period t depends on the value of Y in the previous n periods. The residual or error term, e_t, is the random portion of Y_t and is not explained by the model. This equation is very similar to a regression equation in which previous values of the dependent variable are used as independent variables to explain movements in Y_t.

The moving average model which is another part of Box-Jenkins may be written in the following term

$$Y_t = m + c_1 e_{t-1} + c_2 e_{t-2} + \ldots + c_p e_{t-p} + e_t.$$

Where m stands for the mean of the stationary series and the error terms e_t — i, are the random portions of Y_{t-i}, which is not explained by the autoregressive model.

The autoregressive-moving average model, which is a combination of the two can best be described by

$$Y_t = a_1 Y_{t-1} + a_2 Y_{t-2} + \ldots + a_n Y_{t-n} + C_1 e_{t-1} + C_2 e_{t-2} + \ldots C_p e_{t-p} + e_t$$

In describing their approach to forecasting, Box and Jenkins have divided the forecasting problem into three stages as follows:

(i) *Identification*: Identification is the choice of one or just a few models that seem appropriate for further consideration. With some practice this can be accomplished. It is generally thought to be a good policy, at least, to start with simple, low order models and then move to higher order ones. This logic is based on the more pragmatic reason that a model with few parameters will be more satisfactorily estimated than one having many parameters.

(ii) *Estimation*: Estimation is the procedure of estimating parameters of the model from the data. Once a tentative model has been identified, the parameters of the model are estimated. And once the model has been estimated, forecasting with the model is possible. However, before the model is used, it is important to check the model. This is done by use of diagnostic checks.

(iii) *Diagnostic Checking:* Diagnostic checking is necessary to verify the fact that the model is adequate and complete. There are basically two ways of doing this:

(a) Study the residuals—to see if any pattern remains unaccounted for.

(b) Study the sampling statistics of the current optimum solution to see if the model could be simplified.

No doubt, the Box-Jenkins ARIMA methodology is a powerful model-building technique to time series analysis, but this approach has until recently been used by a very few business forecasters. This is largely because of the expertise knowledge and background that is required for applying the technique. It cannot be applied meaningfully unless it is well understood. In addition, management is found reluctant to use this technique as forecasters have met with some resistence in attempting to convince management to go in for this technique. It is too cumbersome to use on the sides of handling and computation. It also requires experience and good judgement for the process of identification of the model. But now indications are that due to the advent of computer technology and packaged computer programmes, this technique would gain popularity and acceptability among the forecasters and management. It is hoped that this technique would be widely used as management becomes more familiar with its advantages.

4.5 Barometric Forecasting Technique

Barometric forecasting is an old technique of forecasting. This is also known by the name of leading indicators forecasting. There is evidence to show that this barometric or leading indicators approach to business forecasting is nearly as old as business itself. More than two thousand years ago merchants used to take the arrival of trading ships as indicators of business activity. Leading indicators have their origin in the continuing quest among forecasters for signs that supposedly will show ahead of time as what is going to happen to the business or an economy. At macro level, a leading indicator is, therefore, a measure of the economy that moves in the same manner as the economy but does so several months ahead of the economy. Its function of moving ahead of the economy, as a whole, is responsible for its designation as 'leading'. It is to be emphasized that leading indicators are essentially an outgrowth of the study of business cycle thruugh the study of statistical time series.

Although the concept of leading or barometric forecasting is not new, as indicated earlier, but the present analysis of barometric forecasting is based largely on the work done at the National Bureau of Economic Research (U. S. A.) by Burns, Moore, Shiskin, and Mitchell. The barometric forecasting model which they have developed is used primarily to identify potential future changes in general business conditions, rather than conditions for a specific industry or firm. The number of series selected by them, using both observed empirical behaviours and theories of the business cycle, proved to be fairly reliable indicators of business activity. The list containing leading indicators was presented by Henry Morgenthau in late 1937 and was published in 1938. This list has suggested three classes of indicators : leading, coincident and lagging—and this system of classification is still used by the National Bureau, although the economic variables used in the list have undergone a change in subsequent years. In recent years, the barometric approach to forecasting has been refined greatly, primarily through the work of the National Bureau of Economic Research and the U.S. Department of Commerce. *Business Conditions Digest,* a monthly publication of the Department of Commerce, provides extensive data on a large number of business indicators. Table 4.9 lists twenty-five leading, coincident and lagging economic time series indicators. This is a short list having 12 leading, 7 coincident and 6 lagging indicators. Such long comprehensive list contains 111 (1977) indicators series classified under different economic headings.

The behaviour of these indicators has been illustrated in Figure 4.2.

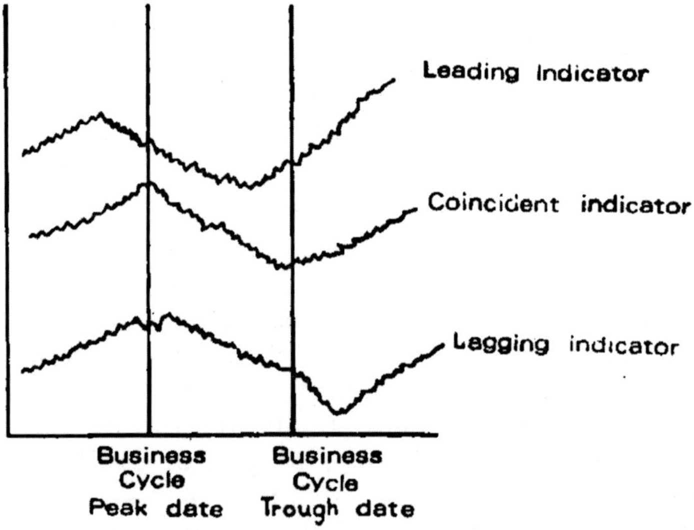

Fig. 4.2. Barometric Indicators

Table 4.9: Leading, Coincident and Lagging Economic Time Series

Leading indicators

Average work week of production workers, manufacturing

Average weekly initial claims—State unemployment insurance

Index of net business formation

New orders—durable goods industries

Contracts and orders-plant and equipment

New building permits—private housing

Change in manufacturing and trade inventories

Industrial materials prices

Stock prices—500 common stocks

Corporate profits, after taxes

Ratio of price to unit labour cost

Manufacturing changes and Consumers instalment debt.

Roughly Coincident Indicators

Employees on non-agricultural pay-rolls

Unemployment rate—total

GNP in current dollars

Industrial production

Personal income

Manufacturing and trade sales

Sales of retail stores

Lagging Indicators

Unemployment rate—15 weeks and over

Business expenditures—new plant and equipment

Book value—manufacturing and trade inventories

Labor cost per unit of output —manufacturing

Commercial and industrial loans outstanding

Bank rates on short-term business loans

As mentioned earlier, barometric, or indicator forecasting is based on the observation that there are lagged relationships between many economic time series. That is, changes in some series appear to follow consistently changes in one or more other series. The rationale for the use of many of these series listed in this Table should be obvious. Many of these series represent commitments to future levels of economic activity. Building permits precede housing starts, and orders for durable goods precede these actual production. An index of common stock prices, for example, is a good leading indicator of general business activity.

Reverting back to the classification, the leading indicator series are those that might be expected to turn before the aggregate economy. So, if some of these series are observed to make clear turn, this could suggest that a turning point for the whole economy is round the corner. The 'roughly coincident' indicators turn at about the same time as the aggregate economy measures, but sometimes series figures are related quickly after the date to which they relate. Therefore, when many of these coincident indicators seem to be changing in direction, this is taken to be the proof that a turn has already occurred in the economy. The lagging indicators are series that react slowly to changes of direction in the main part of the economy. Therefore, if changes are explained in these lagging series, it becomes more or less certain that a turning point has occurred in the recent past. The lagging series are thus used largely to confirm what the other indicators have been suggesting, if there is nothing wrong with the working of the system. The leading indicators, as a whole, are found considerably more volatile than the coincident or the laggers. The swings in the former, during upswing and downswings, are virtually always greater than those in the leaders, is less than in the coincident, and growth in the laggers is greatest of all.

It may be mentioned that a careful following of statistical indicators reflecting the economy within the three classification framework emphasizes the complex nature of the movements in the economy and also helps to deal with such a complexity. This gives a better idea as where the economy had been, where the economy is, and where it is going The idea 'where the economy is going* is an essential ingredient in forecasting.

Like other forecasting techniques, there are also some problems in achieving barometric forecast.

Firstly, few series always correctly indicate changes in another economic variable. Even the best series exhibit only 80 to 90 percent accuracy.

Secondly, even the indicators with good records of forecasting, directional changes, more often, fail to lead by a consistent period. If a series is to be a good barometer it not only must indicate directional changes but, additionally, must provide a constant lead time. The test of lead time consistency is met by few series.

Thirdly, barometric forecasting provides very little information about the magnitude of change in forecast variable though it may be satisfactory from the standpoint indicating directional change with a stable lead time.

Fourthly, forecaster often faces a dilemma concerning which indicator to believe when some are signaling a change in overall economic activity while others are not. Many studies have been made to test the theory of barometric indicators. It was found that the National Bureau's leading indicators do lead, but often by a less extent than suggested by a National Bureau analysis and not in a consistent fashion.

Fifthly, another basic limitation of the indicators is that they are selected mainly in keeping in view their historical performance. But the relationship among various indicators cannot be considered as stable ones. Their timing patterns will change with change in the structure of the economy, in consumors' preferences and in the reactions of business and government to changing business conditions.

Lastly, it is argued that the evaluation and selection methods used by the National Bureau have not been sufficiently sophisticated. And the superior indices and other ways of distilling the relevant information, undoubtedly, contained in the indicators, could be devised. Until this is done, the present method, no doubt, will continue to have a significant place to occupy in the field of forecasting, but with all its drawbacks.

4.5.1 *Composite and Diffusion Indexes.* In order to overcome the difficulties in barometric forecasting technique, composite and diffusion indexes have been devised. Composite indexes are weighted averages of several leading indicators. This index attempts to deal with situation when some series exhibit large movements while other series are far less volatile. If we take percentage changes in each series, then this index will convert all changes to a common denominator, that is, percent of change. It must, however, be remembered that the usefulness of index depends on the experience and judgement of the forecaster.

Diffusion indexes are similar to composite indexes. This copes with the problem of differing signals given by the indicators. It gives the percent of indicators that are rising during the period in question. In making computation of a diffusion index for a group of indicators, we give 1 to a series that is rising, 1/2 to a series that is unchanged, and zero to a series that is falling. For example, if 15 individual indicators have proved to be reliable leading indicators of cement sales, a diffusion index would give the percentage of these indicators which are increasing at the present time. Suppose, 5 are rising, the diffusion index would be fifth-fifteenths or 33.33 percent. The range of the index can be set from 0 to 100, with 50 representing a neutral mid-point indicative of a balance in expansive and contractive forces at work in the business system as a whole. Typically, the index will be declining from the high portion of this range towards the mid-point well before the onset of recession, and will be rising from the lower portion of the range towards the midpoint well before the actual transition from recession to recovery in the economy as a whole. The crossing of the mid-point is logically an event in the index which indicates the reversal of cyclical phase. Diffusion indexes may be constructed using any combination of indicator series which according to forecaster is appropriate. The most comprehensive diffusion index constructed by the NBER (U.S.A.) includes some 400 series that are generally in conformity with business cycle patterns.

Basic limitation of diffusion indexes is that these indexes are, by their nature, limited statistical tools marked by a considerable abstraction from reality. Diffusion indexes cannot appropriately recognize a number of impending events which more general forecasting approaches can specifically embody. Despite this shortcoming, the diffusion index approach to forecasting is now widely accepted as a useful supplementary way of obtaining the breadth and vigour of a business cycle movement.

In summary, barometric forecasting may provide a better forecasting than several naive techniques. But even with the use of composite and diffusion indexes, the barometric forecasting technique is considered a poor tool of forecasting. It is not suitable for all forecasting problems. It is generally used as input for forecasts of aggregate economic variable. The technique cannot substitute for less mechanical, more judgemental techniques of forecasting that will permit freer play to experience and judgement.

4.6 Cycle Forecasting for the Individual Business

It is an accepted fact that business cycles have a bearing on many industries and individual organizations. Business cycles have received attention since the very beginning of the economic system. Consequently, now there are various theories which can explain the causes of the occurrence of business cycles, in economic and business activities. Whatever the explanation, business cycles do take place. For the purpose of forecasting, we consider only two possible causes of the business cycles, viz., capital spending and inventory levels. Reduction in capital spending will slowdown in economic activity. Reduction in capital spending occurs when recession is predicted in the economy. Similarly, expansion in capital spending would occur during boom. These factors must be considered while preparing forecast. The level of inventories, which would fluctuate depending on the situation, has deep effects on the cycle as well as implications for sales forecasting when the cycle changes. It must be kept in mind while preparing forecasts aimed at predicting the cycle that such adjustments in inventories are a major element in determining the time of turning points in the cycle. No doubt, predicting the cycle is a complex task that requires stupendous efforts and authentic information. As far as possible, underestimation or over-estimation of the magnitude of changes in periods of boom and recessions, should be avoided.

Steps in Pressure Calculations. The cycle forecasting approach is also known as 'pressures' analysis. The procedure which is relatively straightforward is explained here. For preparing the cycle analysis, a 12 month moving total of the series is computed.

The yearly total for the year 1985 is given opposite the last month, i.e., December (col. 4). Similarly, the rest 12 months moving totals can be found out by dropping the earliest month and adding the most recent month. This process is to be repeated and thus seasonally in the data is eliminated.

Table 4.10: Computing Pressures for Business Cycle Forecasting

1 Year	2 Months	3 Actual Orders	4 12 Month Moving Totals (M.M.T.)	5 Ratio of 12 Month Moving (12/12) Totals
1985	Jan.	110		
	Feb.	160		
	March	180		
	April	170		
	May	205		
	June	200		
	July	195		
	Aug.	201		
	Sep.	190		
	Oct.	202		
	Nov.	203		
	Dec.	206	2222	
1986	Jan.	209	2321	
	Feb.	270	2431	
	March	265	2516	
	April	285	2631	
	May	265	2691	
	June	255	2746	
	July	245	2796	
	Aug.	276	2871	
	Sept.	300	2981	
	Oct.	305	3084	
	Nov.	310	3191	
	Dec.	315	3300	148.5
1987	Jan.	260	3351	144.4
	Feb.	290	3371	138.7
	March	280	3386	134.6
	April	295	3396	129.1
	May	300	3431	127.5
	June	305	3481	126.8
	July	250	3486	124.7
	Aug.	280	3490	121.6
	Sept.	320	3510	117.8
	Oct.	360	3565	115.6
	Nov.	380	3635	113.9
	Dec.	449	3769	114.2

In the next column (col. 5), the ratios of the 12 month moving total to the 12 M. M. T. of a year are given. These ratios when multiplied by 100 are given in the final column of the Table, where each 12/12 pressure is listed opposite the M. M. T. used as the numerator in the ratio. Thus, the 12/12 for December 1986 is obtained by taking the 12 month moving total for December 1986, dividing it by the 12 month moving total for December 1985, and multiplying by 100. The resulting 12/12 value indicates that the 12 month moving total has increased by 48.5 over its year earlier value. Similarly, other values in this column are obtained.

A close scrutiny of the 12/12 pressure of monthly orders in the Table indicates that a minimum value for that ratio was in November, 1987, indicative of the bottom of the cycle. It must be mentioned that we can use any number of periods for computing pressures. Generally the values 1/12, 3/12 and 12/12 are used in computing pressures. We can also use the same approach in calculating pressures with any kind of time series.

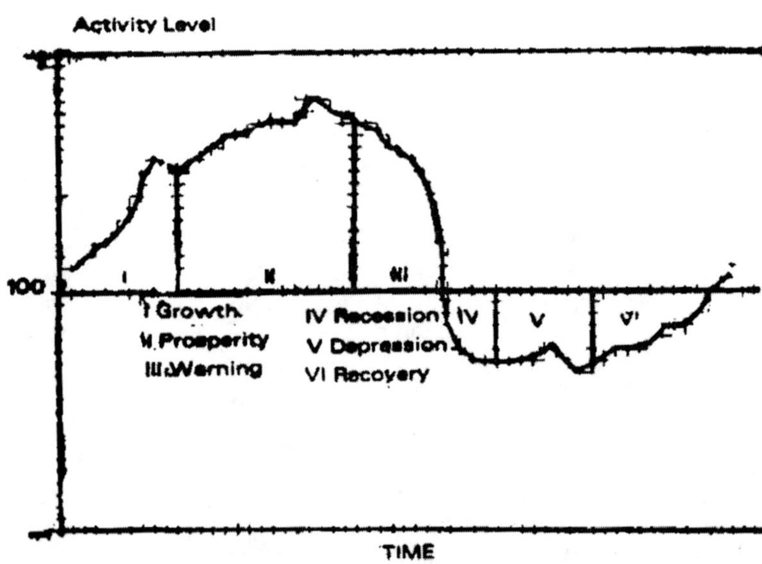

Fig. 4.3: Six Phases of a Bussiness Cycle

It is interesting to see that planning management actions can be based on pressure cycle forecasts described earlier. For some business which are cyclical in nature, it becomes necessary to fit the stage of business cycle in which it finds itself. Business cycles can be conveniently divided into six major phases such as growth, prosperity, warning, recession, depression and recovery, (see Figure 4.3 and Table 4.11). And once it is agreed that a business generally goes through these phases of a cycle, then the management task is to determine appropriate action for any given phase, on the basis of the forecasting movement, through these phases. The suggested actions are listed in Table 4.11.

While concluding, it may be repeated that it becomes easy for the management, through pressure cycle analysis, to identify a particular phase of business cycle well in advance and to take suitable and appropriate action for

Table 4.11: Planning for the Six Phases of a Business Cycle

Sr. No.	*Phase*	*Actions*
1.	Growth	Expand workforce, Accelerate training, Expand plant, Examine outside manufacturing sources, Build up inventories.
2.	Prosperity	Stay in stock, Review sales forecasts, Freeze plant expansions and unload surplus equipments.
3.	Warning	Reduce inventories, Start cuts in training and advertising, Weed out bad products, Cut hiring, Reduce long term purchasing commitments.
4.	Recession	Further inventory reduction, Layoffs, Review purchase decisions.
5.	Depression	Freeze workforce, Keep skilled employees, Reduce work hours if needed, Order major capital equipments for next upswing, Enter into long-term leases and labour contracts, Prepare training programmes.
6.	Recovery	Re-hire Build inventories, Get distributors to build inventories.

the organization for any given phase, So the job of the forecaster is to indentify the phase in which the business now finds itself and to suggest suitable actions to the management accordingly.

PART THREE

Part Three is devoted to the discussion of some important qualitative forecasting techniques in a systematic and orderly manner. Thus, there is obvious departure in this Part from Part Two where all the techniques discussed were quantitative in nature. The techniques which imply the use of judgemental factors, experience and knowledge in arriving at a forecast are frequently referred to as qualitative techniques. The term qualitative is used to denote a forecasting technique focussed primarily on predicting the environment and technology over the long period. In these forecasting techniques, as indicated, knowledge and information rather than some set of mathematical rules play dominant role. While attempting these methods, a selective approach has been adopted which admittedly does not describle every technique found in the literature of forecasting. Thirteen such techniques which are considered more important have been analyzed It is made clear in the very outset that the space devoted to a technique is not necessarily an indication of its importance.

For the sake of convenience and also on account of their distinct characteristics, these techniques can be classified into two categories viz., subjective and technological forecasting. All technological forecasting techniques further have been sub-divided into two subgroups viz., the exploratory and normative techniques. These techniques enable the forecaster to extend the boundaries of thinking and are found to be very useful. But the basic difficulty associated with these techniques is that different experts using the same method do not always produce the same forecast. Sometimes difference in opinion may be very wide leaving one in utter confusion as to which technique is right and which is wrong.

Chapter Five

Qualitative Forecasting Techniques (I) (Subjective Assessment Techniques)

There are number of situations in economics, business and other fields which cannot be tackled with the quantitative forecasting techniques. In many such cases, the quantitative data may neither be available nor relevant. For instance, the manager who is interested in the forecasting of cost of a product may have sufficient data on past sales of the product, but this data is rendered irrelevant due to the introduction of a new competitor's product in the market. Similarly, historical data is not just available when the forecasting is to be done for the new product. Under such situation, manager cannot make use of the past or historical data for the purpose of developing forecasting. But manager at the same time is faced with the problem of making available a forecast required for decision making. How can he surmount this type of difficulty? This is possible through the use of qualitative forecasting. In order to tackle all such and other similar cases, qualitative forecasting techniques are required. As mentioned earlier, knowledge and information rather than some set of mathematical rules are needed in these techniques. All these techniques (qualitative) can be classified into two broad categories viz., Subjective Assessment Methods and Technological Methods. Subjective Assessment Methods will be described in this chapter. The other category of technological forecasting techniques will be dealt with in subsequent Chapter Six.

In case of subjective techniques, subjective assessment of the situation is made. Some of the more popular subjective assessment techniques are: Survey and opinion polling techniques, market experimentation, executive opinion, sales-force polling and probability forecasting techniques. All these techniques are now discussed turn-by-turn in the following pages.

5.1 Survey and Opinion Polling Techniques

Survey and opinion-polling techniques are very useful forecasting tools particularly in making short period forecasts. The use of survey in business forecasting, a phenomenon of the postwar era, has grown considerably in the past three decades. Survey techniques may be used for forecasting the overall level of economic activity and also for the individual firm. Survey generally is conducted through personal interview or mailed questionnaire asking business firms, government agencies, and individuals about their future plans. And much of the value to be taken in the future by some economic variable may already have been determined by plans or commitments by the decision making unit. For instance, a household may have decided to buy a new car in six months time and is already adjusting its spending plans accordingly. Similarly, a company is planning to extend its capacity in next year, and is already under the active consideration of the management as how to raise the capital needed for this expansion. Further, firms may be asked about the opinions as what they expect will take place either in the economy at large or in sectors that particularly affect them. The consumers may also have an aggregate opinion about particular phenomenon that is useful for forecast. Similarly, attitudes of the individuals or firms can be assessed towards a particular product or situation. So data on all these aspects can be gathered in a sensible manner and forecasting can be made on the basis of survey of household or firm. It may be mentioned that survey data can either be used directly to form forecast or it can be used simply to expand some information set. It is in the second rule that the main forecasting advantages of survey data can be realized. The rationale for the use of survey and opinion polling techniques is that certain attitudes having an impact on decision may be identified in advance of the actual implementation of the decision. It must, however, be noted that while surveys do provide an alternative to the quantitative forecasting technique, they are generally used to supplement rather than supplant quantitative analysis. The value of survey techniques as a supplement to quantitative method stems from two factors. First, a non-quantifiable psychological element is inherent in most economic and business behaviour, and surveys are particularly well suited to consider this phenomenon. Second, some quantitative model building is done under the assumption of stable past relationships, behaviour and the like. For instance, if consumers tastes are changing, or if businessmen begin to lose confidence in the economy, then survey techniques may be able to unfold these trends. Besides, survey techniques may provide the only source of data in case of a new product. Many useful surveys for forecasting business activity in various sectors of the economy can be made. These can be in the lines of plant and equipment expenditures, inventory changes and sales expectations, consumer expenditures or consumer intentions, sales force polling etc.

But this method sometimes is found lacking in practice. The information elicited from the persons may either be less authentic and limited It is hardly possible in many cases to provide accurate answers to hypothetical questions. To cite an example, if an interviewer asks how would you react to a 5, 6 or 7 percent increase or decrease in the price of a model of car, could you respond correctly, the answer is in the negative. But despite these drawbacks, it is useful tool in the field of forecast. Using subtle enquiries, a trained interviewer can extract a good deal of useful information from the respondents. As indicated earlier, subjective information can be obtained only through the media of interview, and surveys represent a most important body of economic business intelligence for business forecasting. These surveys do have forecasts values but should be interpreted and used carefully. In the end, it must also be warned that surveys which are useful for short-term forecasts are of little use in the preparation of long-term forecasts.

5.2 Market Experimentation

Market experiment technique involves examining consumer behaviour in actual market situation. To illustrate, think of a firm which finds one or more markets for its product with some well defined characteristics, and then prices, advertising, and other controllable variables used in the demand function are varied hoping to get favourable reactions from the consumers either over time or between markets. In order to measure the impact, the company would be required to keep weekly or monthly record of price changes and other data, and then see how these changes affect demand of the product of the firm. If the markets are separate and located geographically at different places, then the firm will also determine how these characteristics as income, family size, educational level and others affect the level of demand. The final results are then utilized to generate demand forecasts for the firm's product.

This method of forecasting though useful, is not without some serious limitations.

Firstly, skill is required in designing market research studies that will reveal above mentioned relationships and determine their validity. It may happen sometimes that a single factor may upset an otherwise strong correlation between variables. So there is a need to use some trick to recognize and make correction for such factors.

Secondly, market experimentation is quite an expensive affair and is, therefore, usually undertaken on a scale too small to allow high levels of confidence in the results. Quite related to this problem is the one of short-run-versus long-run effects. Market experiments are rarely run for sufficiently long periods to suggest the long-run effects of various price, advertising and packaging strategies. Thus, the forecaster is compelled by circumstances to examine short-run data with the intention to use and extend it for a larger period of time.

Thirdly, uncontrolled parts of the experiment may pose some problems particularly where there are significant changes in economic conditions during the period of experimentation. For example, a change in competing product's expenditure, price, or packaging may invalidate the results. There is also additional fear of losing the customers as a result of price manipulation during the time of experimentation and which may not be regained after the experiment is over.

Happily, there is also available a second market experimentation procedure which is known as laboratory experiment technique or a "Consumer Clinic". This technique, to a greater extent, is free from the weakness found in earlier methods of market experimentation. Under this method consumers are given funds with which to "Shop" in a simulated store. With this method, experimenter can learn many things about consumer's behaviour by varying prices, product packaging, display, and other factors. This technique has the advantage over field experiments for this has greater control of extraneous factors and its cost is also somewhat lower. But the basic shortcoming associated with this method is that the consumers may well distort their shopping habits as they are aware that they are part of an experiment. Also due to cost consideration, the size of sample cannot be reasonably large rendering the inference drawn from the sample to the universe/population quite dubious. All this tends to obviate the use of this technique in forecasting.

In summarising, it may be commented upon that market experimentation technique provides some useful information for building up a forecasting system. But the high cost and the uncontrollable factors which are parts of this experiment are its basic drawbacks. Clearly, the market research technique of forecasting can be recommended when its utility exceeds its cost.

5.3 Jury of Executive Opinion Technique

Jury of Executive Opinion Technique is one of the simplest and most widely used forecasting techniques available. This technique is used more often on a micro level within the firm for forecasting sales. Under this system, the subjective views of top management are averaged to generate one forecast about future for the item to be forecast. The procedure is very simple. The top executives sit around a table and decide as a group what their best estimate is for the item to be forecast. A company generally invites together executives from sales, production, finance, purchasing and administrative departments for their opinion. The opinion of all may then be averaged to arrive at a most representative opinion for forecast. If the jury varies greatly in opinion then the members of the jury are asked to submit their estimates in writing, later to be reviewed by the president or vice-president, as the case may be, of the jury. He will then make the final assessment after taking into account the views expressed by all the members. The president or vice-president may also modify the resulting forecast based on his own expectations and insights.

The major advantages which are often cited in support of this approach are (i) that it supplies forecast quickly and without much difficulty, (ii) that this method brings together a variety of specialized ideas, and (iii) it may be the only feasible means of forecasting under certain situations. This is particularly the case when there is absence of data of the item to be forecast. Despite the usefulness and straight-forwardness of the technique, it is not without drawbacks.

The main drawback of the method is that appropriate weight may not be assigned to the viewpoint expressed by an executive who is not of great standing in the organization. The weights assigned to each executive's assessment will depend, to a greater extent, on the position and personality of that executive in the organization. Another drawback of this method is that judgement plays an important role in it and judgement or opinion sometimes may be inferior to the fact based on quantitative information. Finally, it also involves costly executive time, and it is also difficult to breakdown the forecasting in a detailed manner in terms of product, market etc. All the above factors tend to render forecasting based on opinion somewhat defective and impracticable.

5.4 Sales Force Foiling

This technique is generally used for making sales forecasting of the firm. Under this method, the firm gathers views of their own salesmen regarding their expectations for future sales by specific geographical area and product line. Naturally, it is considered and rightly too that the men who are closest to the ultimate customers may feel the nurves of the customers and have greater insights regarding the state of the future market. The process of preparing forecasts under this method is described below. Each salesman will estimate the probable sales in his or her territory, keeping in view the annual budgeting and planning cycle of the company. After collecting information individually, this is forwarded to the central office for composite forecasting for the particular area, region or district. Generally, the details—geographical area, product line, customer size, and so on, are given in a detailed manner for its suitability for practical purposes. To ensure greater accuracy there is often superior staff to cross check the genuineness of the individual sales persons' estimates. Sometimes forecasts based on sales-force polling may be used to modify other quantitative forecasts which have been developed internally in the firm.

The major argument which is advanced in favour of this method is that it is based on the specialized knowledge of the salesmen who are closest to the market place. This will ensure fair amount of correctness and authenticity in estimates. The disadvantages of this approach are quite similar to those found in the forecast based on consumer surveys. Sometimes sales people prove to be very poor estimators. They may be unaware of the economic situations or patterns that may affect demand violently which makes their sales estimate awry and void.

There is also an alternative to the sales force polling approach. The alternative is known by the name 'sales management technique.' Under this technique, the specialized knowledge of the sales executive staff is taken rather than assessment by individual salespeople at the grassroots level. The major advantage of this approach in comparison with sales force approach lies in the fact that the former short cuts the time required to obtain the sales forecasts.

5.5 Subjective Probability Forecasting

It is to be remembered and emphasized that a comprehensive forecast should contain the element of probability—one of the four elements present in a comprehensive forecast. This role of probability in forecasting has been recognized by many. Through the use of probability one can deal squarely with the element of uncertainty in management decision making. This technique approaches the problem of forecasting through a different angle. It does not specify a forecast in terms of single number but within certain limits which may be called probability limits. For instance, the company might like to specify three or four different levels of sales covering the full range of possible outcomes, and might then assess subjectively the probability associated with achieving each level of outcome. Thus probability turns out to be an integral part of forecasting under such situations. But to fix the probability level is not an easy and straight-forward task. This task further gets complicated as there may be complete lack of historical statistics of the phenomenon or event which may take place only once a while. Not only this, the problem is further aggravated as there are bound to be a chain-like sequence of events making it difficult to estimate. Under these conditions, forecaster is confronted with uncertainty at many stages and it becomes very difficult for him to develop any worth-while forecast.

Let us now, with this background, illustrate the forecasting technique by using probability. At the first stage personal opinions for forecasting probability, which is related to the description of the degree of probability, is generated. Views may be expressed in narrative or descriptive terms. The probabilities are denoted by a percentage figure or a number on the scale 0 to 1.0 so that

100% would correspond to certainty, and

90% „ ,, ,, a most probable outcome,

while 10% „ ,, ,, an unfavourable outcome, and

0% „ ,, ,, impossible.

Actually, there are many other types of scales to cover the probabilities which can be used. Following chart gives one such scale.

Descriptive version	*Percentage*	*Odds*	*Probability*
Highly probable	90-100%	10 to 1 on	0.90
Quite probable	75-90%	3 to 1 on	0.75
As probable as not	50%	evens	0.50
Not very probable	10-25%	4 to 1 against	0.20
Highly improbable	0-10%	10 to 1 against	0.10

It would be convenient if one proceeds with only five classifications, although more classifications or sub-divisions are possible to make. No doubt, a detailed classification would improve the sophistication but at the same time would make the procedure quite cumbersome and unwieldy. To assign probability values in terms of the classification is difficult task even for the expert in the field. But more often these values have turned out to be true. An example may be cited in support of this assertion. The experts of the American moon project, Appollo, set the probability factor for safety of 99.9 percent and 90 percent chance of success—both values were laid down five years before the three men actually landed on the surface of the moon.

Probability assessment can also be made through building up of cumulative probabilities. This method can be developed step-wise as under :

(a) Call for two dates corresponding to 0.1 and 0.9 probabilities.

(b) Ask for the intermediate date corresponding to a probability of 0.50.

(c) Ask for other intermediate values on either side of 0.50 for example, 0.25 and 0.75.

In order to develop probability distribution, let us assign equal probabilities over a specified future years. Then the first question would be asked whether the two points of time (two extremes) have the same probabilities as the middle three. If the opinion is expressed that the middle three are two times more likely than the extremes, the values would be changed as under:

	1	*2*	*3*	*4*	*5*
Start	0.200	0.200	0.200	0.200	0.200
1st change	0.125	0.250	0.250	0.250	0.125

(In possible events in a given situation, the sum of the probabilities assigned to each of these individual event must be exactly equal to *1)*

Then the next question arises whether the middle values are equal or different. The outcome of the change would be:

2nd change	0.125	0.150	0.300	0.300	0.125

Similarly, a third change could be made by asking whether one of the third or fourth values should rank the higher :

3rd change	0.125	0.150	0.350	0.250	0.125

In this manner, the first stage of intuitive judgement applied to the probability forecasting of single event leads to cumulative probabilities in which confusions between probability and time, or some other parameter, are developed. The use of Delphi technique discussed in the next chapter takes this method still further where it would be possible to compare probabilities between various events and obviously would take us to the position where the relationship between time, probability and other parameters would be more harmoniously understood.

To what extent probability procedure of forecasing should be refined actually depends on the forecast topic. It is desirable to have elaborate methods for the major studies at high organizational or national levels when significant decisions are stipulated. Otherwise for lower level studies simpler forecasting technique will do.

Chapter Six

Qualitative Forecasting Techniques-II (Technological Techniques)

Forecasting for technology is an important aspect for planning and expansion of the organization. Thus, it is highly desirable that technology forecasting be introduced as an integral part of the planning process. Technological forecasters are concerned with the development of various technologies that wilt be at a particular time in future. The interest of the organization lies in deciding whether it should exploit the technological opportunities indicated by the forecasts. Technological forecasting can be done at both the national and corporate level. Technological forecasting can further be sub-divided into two types viz., (i) Exploratory techniques and (ii) Normative techniques. Both the types, as promised earlier, are discussed in the present chapter.

6.1 Exploratory Forecasting Techniques

Exploratory forecasting is that which starts with the knowledge and assessment of the past and seeks to forecast the future on that basis. The exploratory techniques which have been studied in this chapter include Brain storming, Scenario development, the Delphi approach, Curve fitting, Analogy, Morphology and Gap analysis.

6.1.1 *Brain Storming.* The technique of brain storming was developed by Osborn in the year 1938. He described this technique in his book entitled *Your Creative Power and Applied Imagination.* The technique is very simple. Under this technique, a specific type of problem is discussed by a group of people with one controller who give their ideas in a spontaneous manner. Not only this, an effort is made to generate further new ideas through interaction within the group. Actually, the aim is to gather the maximum number of ideas no matter they may be wild cat or remote in practice from the real problem. The controller may intervene to make suggestions such as : can we reverse, re-arrange, magnify, reduce, substitute the first ideas? It is the duty of the controller to avoid criticism and judgement at too early a stage. This, of course, comes later in the meeting when the mass of ideas is tailored to solutions of an apparent acceptability which may be only five or ten percent of the original total.

Brain storming addresses mainly to the following questions. The first question is, are we solving the right problem? This question is tackled by stating the problem to be solved and ensuring that the group understands it completely. The next question is, can we break our logical thought patterns? This in fact is the stage which has been subjected to most development and improvement. This can be done by adopting more orderly approach, such as the systematic use of check lists, the examination of sequences so that gaps can be revealed. The next question is: can we become more receptive to new ideas? In brain storming approach, efforts are made to encourage the receptivity of new ideas. Obviously, some of the most important new projects of modern times could easily have been frustrated had initial criticism dominated. Finally, one more question is, how can others help in taking decisions in the matter ?

It is quite possible that in the process of making experiments with this approach of brain storming, some outcomes can be distinctly new and unlikely to have been brought to light by other means. It is an established fact that brain storming has an important place in the field of forecasting. But it always would give good results if it is used alongwith other more systematic method.

Brain storming is applicable to problems arising in a wide range of business and technological areas. It is an apt technique for providing answers to such typical questions as: how do we get ideas for new products/ processes/procedures or services? flow do we get ideas for new uses/outlets or markets, what alternatives are there to this or that type of procedure?

Reverting back to group formation it may be mentioned that it should have, on panel, all types of specialized persons who understand the various aspects of a particular problem. The working group should consist of a chairman or leader and at least five/ six more members so that the influence of dominant personalities is minimized. The chairman or leader of the group, who conducts brain storming session should be experienced one. The chairman in addition to his role as leader, may also contribute to the proceedings during the definition of the problem. But he should avoid prejudicing the process by introducing his own thoughts on the matter. It would be worthwhile that the leader records the views of the members rapidly may be in numerical order. He may use wall or flip charts, or cards to display at all times the accumulation of ideas, thereby adding to the stimulation of thought. Later, these ideas are classified and a series of 'clusters' can be identified.

The application of brain-storming and its related techniques contribute to the first stage in the forecasting of technology—the qualitative element by providing narrative description of a new product or a new process. Brain-storming in one form or another has been employed by the well known 'think tank' units in several countries and at different levels of organization. It can be introduced as a problem solving device in a wide range of business and technological areas. But it should be remembered that it is not very suitable procedure for solving problems which have only one possible answer or for those which are quite complex and diffused.

6.1.2 *Scenario Development.* In recent years, the word scenario has gained wide popularity. A scenario attempts to set up a logical sequence of events to indicate how some future state or situation can be evolved step by step. It describes a future picture of the environment. It has been applied to a variety of forecasting approaches ranging from highly subjective word pictures, aggregation of specific forecasts in an area of study, to complex dynamic models such as those used by Meadows in *The Limits to Growth* study (1972).

Scenario writing takes a well-defined set of assumptions, and then develops an imaginative conception of what the future would look like if these assumptions were true. Actually in this sense, scenarios are not future predictions but rather they present a number of possible alternatives each one based on certain assumptions and conditions. And ultimately, it is for the forecaster to assess the validity of the assumptions in the matter of deciding as which scenario is most likely to occur.

The use of the most probable scenario, or, "surprise free" viewpoint provides a basis against which to collect other alternative scenarios. The main purpose of these scenarios is not strictly to predict the future, as indicated above, but rather to facilitate a systematic exploration of branches or net-work of critical events within some explicit time frame. Scenarios can be prepared either just for specific technologies, such as electricity production, water supply and quality, or military arms development, or for whole societies, such as the Indian economy or the whole world. Scenarios are sometimes written by individual but more recently they have often become team efforts, bringing together opinions of experts in a variety of fields. This is particularly the case when a bundle of alternative scenarios is considered.

Herman Kahn (1976) of the Hudson Institute has done a lot of work on scenario. Over period as long as 200 years, the important issues included in the study are population growth, the availability of scarce resources, economic growth, and the effects of technological innovations. Kahn (1964) and Kahn *et al* (1976) developed a number of alternative scenarios for the world. In one such scenario, they assumed that an arms control agreement between the United States and Russia would be reached and China would follow only a defensive policy, not an offensive one. On the basis of these assumptions, Kahn gave a scenario describing a future political-social environment, following a predictable sequence of developments, constraints and ideologies. On the basis of the set of assumptions, he predicted a future environment that would be highly stable and peaceful. Under a different scenario, Kahn assumed that Russia would lose control over the world communist movement.

While writing scenario, it is usual practice to generate three scenarios. The first scenario assumes that current trends will be maintained into the future without much disturbance. This is popularly called a 'surprise free' scenario. For other two scenarios, (plus two alternatives) sets of assumptions may be taken keeping in view their likelihood and internal consistency and establishing a range either side of the 'surprise free' within which the outcome might be expected to fall with a reasonable degree of confidence. As one progresses into the future, the higher the level of uncertainty and is less likely to conform to the 'surprise free' scenario. Therefore, it becomes necessary to write scenarios for several dates in the future.

There are eight steps involved in scenario forecasting. These are: developing a data base, selecting organizational objectives, evaluate organizational variables, evaluate environmental variables, scenario selection, scenario development, analysis of implications of scenarios and implementation of plan.

Briefly stated, the establishment of an adequate data base for scenario is likely to be a substantial and time consuming task. But this is essentially required. The data base must be comprehensive and elaborate. The objectives of the firm must be set and examined critically to see that the objectives of the organization are consistent with its policy. In the next step, variables which are measurable and which measure the performance of the organization need *to* be selected. With the completion of this step now there is sufficient information for selecting the sets of assumptions for the scenarios. For the 'surprise free' scenario, it can safely be assumed that the future environment will evolve without any significant departure from existing trends. For the alternative scenarios, considerable judgement is required for choosing the set of assumptions. For developing the scenarios, it is important to study the mutual impacts of all the chosen organizational and environmental variables. It is to be mentioned that upto this stage no forecasts have been made. It is now necessary to prepare detailed forecasts for the variables using the most proper technique. These will then form ultimately the basis for writing the scenarios. The scenarios will then be described in narrative form bringing out clearly the assumptions made, the mutual impacts of the variables and supported by detailed forecasts for the variables analyzed. And at this stage the implications of the scenarios in relation to the objectives of the organization and future plans must be viewed.

Talking about the practical applications, most of the published scenarios are of wide ranging 'whole futures' studies concerned more with the future of society on a world or national scale than with the more limited sphere of industrial companies. Therefore, it is understandable that this technique was largely ignored by industry. Although neglected by industry until recently, it is attracting considerable attention now that most companies, facing the traumas of fuel crises are giving greater and greater attention to a longer term future which seems to be shrouded by greater degree of uncertainty than at other time in the past. Many companies are now making experiment with the technique and by all available evidence it seems likely that this interest will continue to grow in future. It is unfortunate, however, to point out that term scenario is used very loosely and often is compared with a little more than a science fiction. Scenario-writing can be of particular use to technological planners which will help them in indicating of the priority to be given to a project.

6.1.3 *The Delphi Approach.* The Delphi is perhaps the most commonly used explorative type of technological forecasting technique. The approach was first developed at RAND corporation in 1963. The purpose of Delphi approach is to exploit the specialized knowledge and judgement of experts to obtain a reliable consensus of opinion that can be used as a future forecast. It is a technique for achieving a structured anonymous interaction between experts using a questionnaire approach with controlled feed-back of information designed to eliminate or reduce the shortcomings which are inherent in face to face meeting. The necessary igredients of the method are a carefully selected group of experts and an organizer. At the first stage, a set of properly worded questions are given to each expert. The questions may be as the following :

What is the probability of a World War occurring in the next 20 years?

When will a reliable automated language translator be available?

To such questions the expert is supposed to give a specific date. An answer of "never" is also permitted. The answer may be any number between 0 and 1 inclusive. After receiving the answers, the organizer would summarise them to know the degree of agreement and disagreement, In order to find these a median year and the two quartiles of the distribution of forecasts are used at the first stage. For example, there are twelve experts who gave following years as the occurrence of a particular event.

1986 '88 '91 ↑ '95 '96 '98 ↑ 2000
First quartile Median
2000 2000 ↑ 2000 2010 never
Last quartile

It is clear that the median lies between 1998 and 2000 and the average of these two years is 1999. The first quartile lies between 1991 and 1995 (1993 average) and the last quartile is between 2000 and 2000 (2000 average). The median guess, or forecast, is thus 1999 and represents an average value, and the inter-quartile range (IQR) is 1993-2000 and is a measure of the extent of agreement or disagreement of the experts.

At the second stage, the results of the survey are sent back to the experts asking to give their opinion. There is no pressure on the experts to change his/her viewpoint around median or quartiles. If the expert wishes to maintain a viewpoint or forecast outside the interquartile range then he/she is invited by the organizer to state briefly the main reasons for sticking so strongly to a particular forecast. At the third stage, the experts are sent a summary of the second stage, their revised aggregate forecasts, plus the summaries of arguments for holding different views, and again they are asked to provide revised forecasts. They are further allowed for sticking a particular forecast. No doubt, the sequence of questioning may continue to other rounds but due to time and cost constraints the sequence stops after three or four rounds. Gordon and Helmer conducted the first original large-scale Delphi experiment at the RAND Corporation around 1965. Toe technique was immediately accepted as being both sensible and useful. Some of the forecasts made by them in 1965 regarding scientific breakthrough are reproduced in Table 6.1.

Table 6.1: The Delphi Forecasts

	Question	*Median*	*Interquartile range*
1.	Economically useful destination of Sea-water	1970	1970-1983
2.	Automated language translators	1972	1968-1976
3.	New organs through transplanting or prosthesis	1972	1968-1982
4.	Reliable weather forecasts	1975	1972-1988
5.	Controlled thermonuclear power	1985	1980-2000
6.	Feasibility of limited weather control	1990	1987-2000
7.	Economically useful farming of ocean to produce at least 20% of world's food	2000	2000-2017
8.	Use of drugs to raise level of intelligence.	2012	1984-2023

It is clear that some of these forecasts are reasonable and optimistic and came out to be true. This confirms that Delphi is a sensible procedure of forecasting. This method can make a major contribution to forecasting technology, particularly when the data for the application of quantitative techniques are lacking.

The success or otherwise of a particular Delphi forecasting surveys depends on the ease with which the panel of experts is selected, the questions formulated, and the arguments summarized. The selection of the panel of experts is critical to the success of the method. It is altogether necessary to define clearly the range of expertise required. Since one is seeking the best opinion available, this would suggest that the ideal panel should be made up of people even from outside the organization. The number of experts is also important. It should be somewhere between 10 to 20. If the number is less, then it would be better for arriving at consensus and also will not make the administration over complex. Actually, number of experts should vary from situation to situation. Privately conducted Delphi would normally have 10-15 experts, but the number for public or national issues may be considerably larger— upto 100 or even more. As to the aspect of structuring questionnaire, care should be taken that questions should be unambiguous— they should be phrased in a manner so that all respondents interpret them the same way. The questions should be unconditional. Since there is a cross-impact between events, the Delphi respondent must be clear about the specific area of enquiry. Only right type of questions need to be asked. Since forecasts are required to assist decision making, care must be taken to ensure that the questions do in fact relate to the problems facing the organization. Lastly, questions should be limited in number and certainly not too many.

It is to be accepted that Delphi has been a controversial technique and has been a subject of continuous attack by academics. One criticism is that most of the experts engaged in Delphi appear to be playing a game rather than thinking seriously about their position, trying to defend their views, or attacking the views of others. Mostly, people are reluctant to change publicly once the opinions are expressed in meeting. But there is also a bandwagon effect. The effect is that a person in a minority position will tend to suppress his opinion in the face of united opposition. Another most general complaint against this method is its often low level of reliability and its oversensitivity of results to ambiguity in the questionnaires. These disadvantages must be weighed against the advantages that can often be achieved through its use.

In conclusion, the Delphi has servived the many criticisms levelled against it and still remains one of the most widely used techniques. The need for a Delphi can arise in a variety of ways. Well constructed Delphi approach has a very important role to play in the field of forecasting particularly for long-range forecasting. But the Delphi should not be regarded as an end in itself, a simple mechanism for providing an authoritative forecast. Rather, it should be regarded as an input to the forecaster. It is of much importance to see that Delphi studies do not suffer from inadequate preparation. vague or ambiguous event statements, unconsidered answers and inefficient feed back. These are the aspects to which the forecaster must pay meticulous attention.

6.1.4 *Curve Fitting.* Curve fitting is generally discussed as a quantitative forecasting technique. But this can also serve effectively as a qualitiatve or technological forecasting technique. However, it should be borne in mind that there are significant differences in these two approaches. This as a quantitative method, curve fitting is done with a view to approximate the basic trend component of a time series. The basis of this type of curve fitting is empirical data which purports to cover several years. On the other hand, in case of qualitative or technological curve fitting the time span is generally much longer.

For technological forecasting, there are several different types of curves which can well be fitted. The S-Curve which is discussed here is one of the most frequently used forms in technological forecasting.

S-Curvb Approach

This is a qualitative curve fitting approach where little historical data is directly required and used. It is largely the expert judgement which is important and required. The simple time series curves imply that past exponential growth can be extended indefinitely into the future. But this is not always true. The exponential time-series describes only a part, the high growth portion of a more generalized curve. It appears quite logical and convincing that the rate of growth will diminish as the limit (physical barrier) is approached. This situation is applicable in case of both technological and non-technological events. Thus, it is expected that a growth curve will follow a path of the form, shown in Fig. 6-1, normally termed as an S-Curvc. There are historical evidences which prove the shape of this curve. The use of S-curve in representing growth can be applied not only to a given product but also to a given technology. The S-Curve has proved so fundamental to growth that it has been used for forecasting in almost every technological field.

As indicated, the S-Curve would follow the pattern suggested in Figure 6.1. It may be mentioned that while exponential curve may adequately describe growth to point x, it becomes increasingly inaccurate beyond that point. The exponential time-series describes only a part, the high

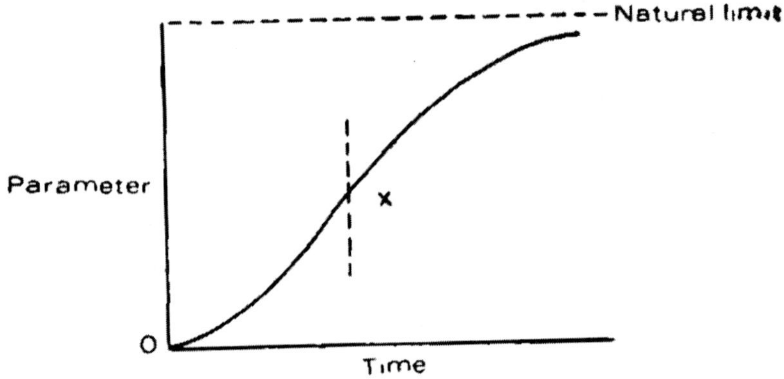

Fig. 6.1: The S–Curve

growth portion of a more generalised curve. An S-Curve, it is evident implies a slow start, a steep growth, and then a plateau. The procedure for establishing an S-Curve is quite identical to that for a single time-series with the additional factor of finding the limiting level. Figure 6.2 shows a 1990 forecast for motor vehicle ownership in a town. No doubt, there is no upper limit set by the laws of nature, nevertheless there are limiting factors determined by socio-politico-economic as well as technological factors in the matter of the ownership of motor vehicle.

It is clear that first part of the S-curve follows an exponential path. But this fast development phase can hardly be sustained as all technologies are finite. And as a matter of fact many business failures have occurred due to non- recognition of S-Curve in business forecasting. Non-recognition of S-Curve is found responsible for incorrect interpretation of the past growth leading to ill-conceived decisions regarding investment which proved disastrous so frequently to the organization.

This method of forecasting provides a more accurate time forecast with a clear indication of the change from growth to maturity with its many planning implications. The signals from S-Curve is often clear and unmistakable. It also forewarns the forecaster to the possibility of a substitute technology.

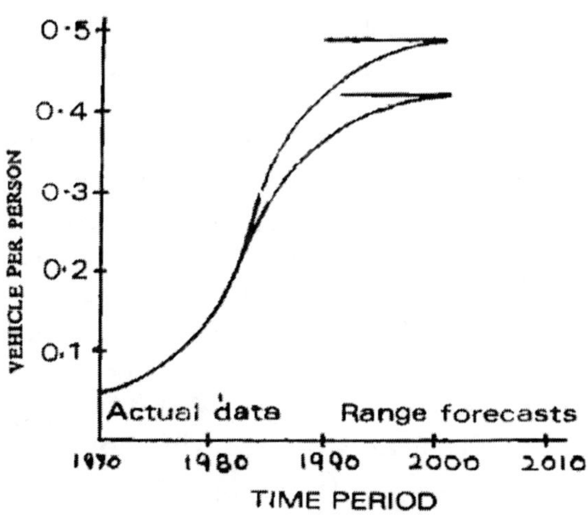

Fig. 6.2: Growth Curve

But the application of S-Curve is not without difficulties. The major difficulty in the use of the qualitative S-Curve is to find the most appropriate type of curve. The solution of this problem depends on the technology or the product one wants to forecast and its characteristics. Besides, expert judgement is also needed. This emphasizes the need for management judgement in checking assumptions and the appropriateness of this method of forecasting in a specific situation.

6.1.5 Analogy Method. Forecasting is also possible by way of i analogy. By studying the analogous situations, the time-table or sequence of events that occurred in the earlier case may be helpful in determining time for the occurrence of the later case. An analogy is an intuitive thought, or chain of thought, about two or more elements (things) which contain similarities based on a key factor identification. The concept is that when two things have been seen to have, at least, one characteristic in com moo, we tend to conclude that an analogy exists. Our interest is then to forecast the probability that they will behave analogously in other respects as well. For example, if we are planning to build from scratch a good quality university to teach 5,000 students, it is worthwhile to look at the experiences of those building a similar university in some other part of the country or even outside the country. No doubt, the forecasts will not be exact because the analogy may not be complete. But all the same this will be very helpful. There are several types of analogies, including technological, historical, biological, geographical and social law analogy. Let us have a bird-eye view of each one of these technological analogies. There are cases of the growth of technology which owe their origin to analogies. A number of examples are taken from aero-space technology to illustrate the 'spin-off' concept as a basis for analogy forecasting. Similarly, there are analogies in engineering and plastics technologies and analogies in chemical and chemical process fields. We now describe briefly the types of analogies referred to above.

(i) *Historical Analogies.* Historical analogies are more intuitive than any of the other forms of this approach. Prediction can be made on what has happened in the past. Examples of the use of historical analogy can be found in the field of weather and stock market. The weather in 1988 for a particular month can be known by comparing the past weather map for similar past of the year. For the stock market, one can plot a stock price index or the price of a particular company's share against time and look for certain patterns. Historical analogies are in fact as old as civilization itself. One major attempt to formalize the use of historical analogies for predictive purposes was made in a book edited by Mazlish (1965). An attempt is made in the book to show a number of analogies between the development of rail-roads and the development of space programme. The effort was to predict the technological development and social and political implications of the space programme by drawing an analogy to these aspects of the development of rail-roads in the last century. Military developments in aircraft to civilian aircraft, computers to pocket calculators and autos in different countries are some other instances of historical analogies.

(ii) *Biological Analogy.* Many researchers have shown that the population growth tends to follow a pattern similar to the growth of biological organism. The same conclusion was reached by Gompertz and Von Bertalanfify. Key features of naturally occurring drugs, insecticides, antibiotics and hormones to the structuring of synthetic analogies, design of synthetic fur and leather products from animal sources, the echo-sounding mechanism of bats, and its jamming by others in relation to radar, wings to air-craft design etc. are some of the analogies which can be cited from biological origins.

(iii) *Geographical Analogy.* Geographical analogy can be used in the sense that similar events in other parts of the world may be found and this can be made the basis of either a casual or a formal analogy. Examples of such analogy are past conquest of land environment by man and the future conquest of the underwater habitat; growth of various consumer's goods in the USA and India; autos and GNP in different countries; effectiveness on crop yield of insecticides in different countries; desalination in arid areas for potable water etc.

(iv) *Social Laws Analogy.* Bell (1964) states that there may be a number of social laws which may predict human behaviour, development of the social environment, and development of political system. Bell, in order to support his thesis used the law of motion of capitalism propounded by Marx. The deteriorating economic condition of labour, the centralization of capital, falling rate of profit, and so on, can work as an analogy to a falling object that accelerates in speed and rate of fall due to the law of gravity. Marx conclusion that capitalism will fall in the same fashion as an object until it crashes, is a sound analogy of this category. This conclusion is based on the natural law which governs the falling object whether they be societies or physical items.

The use of analogies for forecasting is not made, to any practicable extent, by the forecasters. But the use of analogies as a forecasting tool is highly intuitive. Analogies often result from 'applied common sense1, coupled with a good information system covering technological, biological, historical and/or geographical sources. They may be useful in particular situations for which data are not easily available. Since they are to be used intuitively without much effort in many situations, they are preferred to situations where tremendous amount of work is to be done while applying other methodologies more successfully.

For developing the use of analogy, forecaster should aim at to structure the initial stage of the search to satisfy a problem or the need for an innovation. To develop a formal analogy from a casual analogy, following steps may be helpful.

(i) To ascertain the important characteristics, that is, the principles of operation.

(ii) To examine the environment of the analogies. This is absolutely necessary. It should not, however, be assumed that analogies will have perfectly the same outcome in the fields of application. But it will if the key characteristic is found in several environments.

6.1.6 Morphology. The morphological approach to forecasting is perhaps the most systematic. It was introduced first by Zwicky, a Swiss astronomer. He developed it while making efforts to discover new inventions in the field of jet engines. At present, this technique is stated to have more than 30 industrial applications, particularly in new products or new processes.

In the words of Zwicky "Morphological research concerns itself with the development and the practical application of basic methods that will allow us to discover and analyze the structural or morphological inter-relationships among objects, phenomena, and concepts and to explore the results obtained for the construction of sound world". It is evident that the above statement about the method is quite comprehensive and conveys much more than the simple forecasting. It also engulfs in its fold a systematic thinking in solving problems.

There are four basic steps as suggested by Zwicky in developing this forecasting technique :

(i) The statement of the problem which must be formulated and defined very clearly.

(ii) A statement of the essential parameters.

(iii) The construction of matrix based firstly on the essential parameters, and secondly on the alternative means of attaining or satisfying each of the parameters.

(iv) The examination of all the possible permutations of the alternatives.

While making an application of his approach in the late 30s Zwicky identified possible propulsive power plants (Jet engines) that could be activated by chemical energy. In order to define all possible engines of this form, he took following six parameters:

P_1: The medium through which the jet engine moves. There are four components which relate to this parameter, i.e., parameter first (P_1).

P_{12}: denoting that a jet engine moves through a vacuum, *Plt* : denoting that the jet engine moves in the atmosphere,

P_{13}: denoting that the jet engine moves in large bodies of water,

P_{14}: denoting that the jet engine moves in the solid surface strata of the earth.

P_2 : The type of motion of the propellant relative to the jet engine, with the following four components.

P_{21} : denoting a propellant at rest,

P_{22} : denoting a translatory motion,

P_{23} : denoting an oscillatory motion,

P_{24} : denoting a rotary motion.

P_3 : The physical state of the propellant, with the following three components:

P_{31} : denoting a gaseous physical state,

P_{32} : denoting a liquid physical state,

P_{33} : denoting a solid physical state.

P_4: The type of thrust augmentation, with the following three parameters;

P_{41} : denoting no thrust augmentation,

P_{42} : denoting internal thrust augmentation,

P_{43} : denoting external thrust augmentation.

P_5 : The type of ignition, with the following two parameters.

P_{51} : denoting a self-igniting engine,

P_{52} : denoting an externally ignited engine.

P_6: The sequence of operations, with the following two parameters.

P_{61} : continuous operation,

P_{62} : intermittent operation.

It is evident from the above that morphological box or multidimensional matrix of 6 parameters, 576 combinations ($4 \times 4 \times 3 \times 3 \times 2 \times 2 = 576$) of Jet engine can be identified. Obviously, it is not possible to analyze and evaluate all the combinations to achieve a specific set of objectives. So Zwicky had to pick at random some of them for study.

It is interesting that Zwicky, on the basis of morphological study, was able to suggest several new inventions in the jet engine technology and he also earned 16 different patents in this regard. The above example of jet engine is related to advanced technology and is esoteric. The morphological approach can be applied in everyday technological system. In fact, this is the responsibility of R & D personnel who have an obligation to apply morphology to the study of their firm's products and processes.

The major advantage of the morphological approach is that in addition to existing and new system, there may well be a potential for still further systems to be recognized and evaluated. This has found practical applications in the fields like building bricks, spanner-nut and bolt systems, functional fluids, mining and colour television, whole range of food supply system and possible material transformation and clock system. Another advantage of this technique lies in that it allows the user to identify hidden or rare opportunities for technological possibilities those can be profitably developed.

The technique is simple in nature and can prove as a useful tool to the forecaster in many situations. It would be worthwhile if following points are borne in mind by the forecaster while developing the technique.

(i) Reduce the number of basic parameters so that a limited number of concepts emerge.

(ii) Recognize impossible permutations. This will help in understanding the possible combinations. The prior existence of physical or natural constraint may often vitiate the potential of certain combinations.

6.1.7 *Gap Analysis:* Gap analysis is another method of forecasting which is used in a number of management areas. There are two types of gaps viz., market gap and planning gap which can be mentioned. Market gap exists when a segment of consumer is not satisfied with the price, quality, design or volume of the product. The planning gap exists when there is difference between the level of activity aspired by the firm and the level of activity which would be attained. These gaps would offer business and technological opportunities to the organizations.

The idea of gaps as a starting point for forecasting had originated with Jantsch (1972). The concept of gap analysis is, in fact, an interpolative in the sense that it examines a series of products or processes which have an ascending order or performance in order to determine if there remains unknown or unexploited intermediate level. Figure 6.3 below illustrates the concept of interpolative forecasting in a linear system.

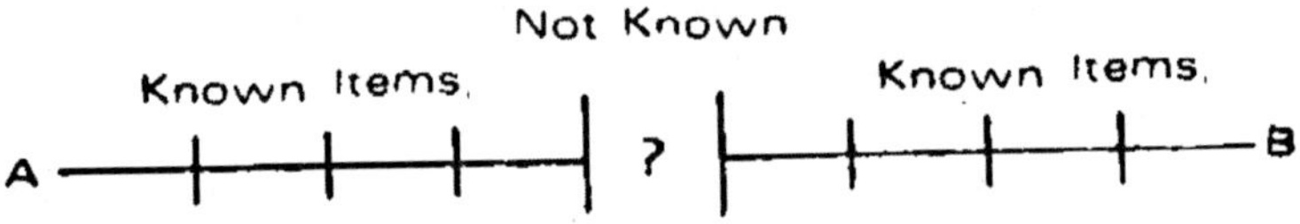

The 'gap' unknown can be fitted in. Actually it was this approach which led to the forecasting of such elements as gallium, germanium and rare gases.

Regarding its practical applications, it can quote various systems or sequences suggesting procedures where gap analysis can be applied usefully. A such well-known sequence is known by the name Fibonacci Numbers. These numbers form a series where every term after the first two is the sum of the preceding two terms. Therefore, if the first two numbers are both unity, the Fibonacci series is:

1 1 2 3 5 8 13 21 34 55 89 144...

This series is found in the life processes of organisms to the design of attractive shapes and forms. We can have some such systems like,

(a) the rate of growth of bees and rabbits,

(b) the branches and scales of pine-apple which grow in Fibonacci sequence. Besides, many geological sedimentary studies are based upon the recognition of gaps occurring in an otherwise well defined series.

Like time series method, it also depends on the availability of a bank of data on existing processes. It also pre-supposes that the key attributes of the processes have been denned and measured appropriately for their completion and orderliness.

6.2 Normative Forecasting Techniques

While developing technology forecast by applying exploratory methods, no attempt was made to incorporate the objective of society or the individual organization. These objectives serve a very important role in determining future developments of the society. Through normative approaches of technological forecasting, these objectives are made an integral part of a forecasting system. Not only this, forecasters have adopted normative methods of technological forecasting in order to overcome some of the difficulties that often prove hindrances in the actual adoption of technology and to make forecast properly when such adoption occurs. There are two such methods: relevance trees and system analysis. This text includes only relevance trees method for its utility and wide-spread adoption.

6.2.1 *Relevance Trees:* The purpose of a relevance tree is to enable the forecaster to examine systematically to select the most appropriate path to the attainment of specified objectives of the organization. The method of relevance tree is not a new technique. Its origin dates back to the development of decision theory and the construction of decision trees which helps the decision maker in selecting the best strategy from among a number of alternatives. Before showing how relevance trees are constructed, the areas where this technique can be applied successfully by the planner are described briefly.

(i) To establish whether a specific normative goal or objective might be achieved. Concise objective setting is the first essential task in relevance tree.

(ii) To determine alternative ways by which the objective might be achieved. There may be a number of alternative routes to the desired end point.

(iii) To establish the need for detailed technology forecasts of the constituent technologies where their performance within the given time scale is critical.

(iv) Selection of an R and D portfolio and selection of technologies to forecast. Technological forecasts are usually more concerned with the accomplishment of specific technological objectives such as air-pollution control.

The best known application of relevance trees is the PATTERN (planning assistance through technical evaluation of relevance numbers) project that has been used by Honeywell Corporation for military space and medical purposes in the mid-1960s. The major objective of this approach is to help planners in identifying the long range development that are required for obtaining the objectives. The computer program used for PATTERN suggests a list of technologies that are essential for achieving these objectives.

One of the first applications of PATTERN was made in U.S.A which evaluated national objectives for military and space explorations. On the top level three goals viz., national survival, creation of credible posture, and favourable world opinion were considered. In order to have rough idea of the possibility of attaining these three goals, a scenario needs to be prepared. Then on the basis of this scenario, a relevance tree was developed by a panel of experts. A relevance tree is prepared which shows major objectives along-with sub-objectives and the level of technologies to meet these.

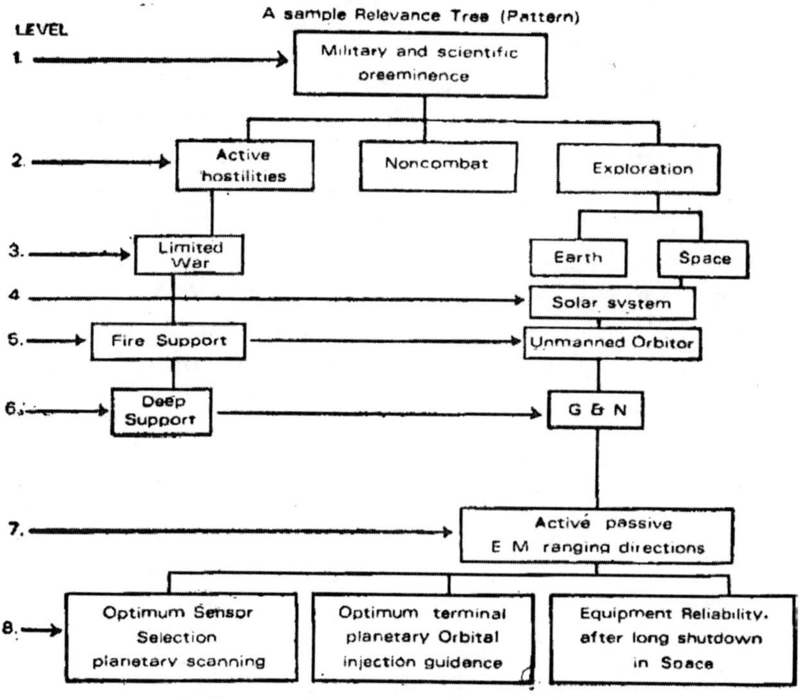

***Fig. 6.4 A Sample Relevance Tree (Pattern)* Note : *Adapted thankfully from Makridakis'* Forecasting**

It is obvious that the elements of the final level represent the breakthrough required for achieving the long range objectives given in the first level. There are many hierarchical levels. In general, the wider the objective the greater the number of levels and complexity of the tree. It is to be noted that once the relevance tree has been prepared then a panel of experts can determine the relevance and the utility of each element of the tree. After receiving answers from the experts the mean of the answers can be computed. Through this process Honeywell could identify a number of missions related to space and ocean exploration, arms control, and so on. Then these missions could be used as the basis for allocating resources, to meet, in a better way, the existing goals. With this approach, lower costs and better performance can be affected. The process of constructing and evaluating the tree is often of greater value than the results of the quantitative evaluation.

Forecasters may be recommended to use this technique. Relevance trees can be used for evaluating a wide range of projects. But it must be realized that the cost of applying this methodology can be significant. It also requires considerable human resources. Not only this, more complicated calculations found in some of the applications do lose touch with reality. It is to be seen that calculations do not assume a spurious respectability which may not be justified by the quality of the data. So, care must be taken that it does not make it complex unnecessarily.

PART FOUR

Part Four through its sole Chapter Seven has been organized into four camponents each examining an important issue. First issue is related to the choosing of an appropriate forecasting technique. Closely associated with this issue, the data requirement and its handling in forecasting is also highlighted. It is emphasized that the quality of data is important in determining the accuracy, credibility and value of a forecast. Also, the controversial aspect— management versus forecaster is touched upon and resolved. The second issue is related to the integration of forecasting with planning and decision making. Understandably, forecasting must be a part of systematic management planning in an organization. The forecasting has a linkage with planning and this role too has been stressed here.

The third issue that of judgemental factor in forecasting is dealt with though briefly. Judgement is critical in determining the success or failure of the forecasting, no matter what method is used. It has been advocated that judgemental factor should be blended with formal factor so that this factor gets reflected even with purely formal techniques. Finally, the role of computer in the field of forecasting, as the fourth issue, is discussed. The cost of using computer is quite tremendous and prohibitive. Therefore, the expenditure on computer in forecasting must be carefully weighed against current and potential benefits arising out of its use.

Chapter Seven

Managing A Forecasting System

7.1 Choosing a Forecasting Technique

The preceding chapters have introduced a variety of forecasting techniques. They range from the highly sophisticated to the very simple from the sublime to the ridiculous. So, it is appropriate to consider, at this stage, the factors which govern the choice of forecasting method for use in a given situation. The important factors in making this choice are viewed as under.

Lead Time : It is the length of time into the future for which forecasts are required. The length of time for the purpose is generally divided into four as under:

(i) Immediate term : less than one month
(ii) Short term : one to three months
(iii) Medium term : three months to two years
(iv) Long term : more than two years

It may be clarified that the exact length of time for each of these four categories varies from one organization to another organization and from one situation to another situation. It is accepted without any dispute that some forecasting techniques are more appropriate for a short lead time and others for a long lead time. For example, for simple exponential smoothing, decomposition and Box-Jenkins immediate period is more relevant. For short term, almost all the techniques have been found to be used.

For medium and long term, multiple regression, econometric and multivariate Box-Jenkins techniques are found to be more suitable. And for very long term forecasts, qualitative methods are preferred over all quantitative methods of forecasting.

Time to Prepare Forecast: The various forecasting techniques differ in the time taken to collect the required data, analyze them, and prepare the forecasts. It is clear tbat a forecast must be ready well in advance otherwise there is no point in preparing for forecast for decision making. Therefore, some forecasting techniques are found to be practically unsuitable when forecasting is needed urgently. Under such circumstances, simple forecasting techniques are only the alternative as they can be prepared in no time. The preparation of forecasting becomes even more difficult when there are numerous items to be forecasted. For the application of forecasting in terms of time from the shortest to longest, the order is : simple exponential smoothing, decomposition, multiple regression, Box-Jenkins, multivariate Box-Jenkins and econometric technique.

Level of Details: While making selection of a forecasting technique, one must be aware of the level of details that will be required for that forecast to be useful in taking decisions. The decision making process is usually sub-divided by many organizations according to the level of details available. For example, the information is required for individual products and their individual styles for planning at the aggregated production level.

Pattern of Data: Pattern of data is very important consideration in making choice of a forecasting method to be used. This is owing to the fact that different forecasting methods vary in their ability to identify different patterns. In case of quantitative methods of forecasting, each technique does make explicit assumption about the type of underlying data pattern. There are four basic sub-patterns of the data. These are: trend, horizontal, seasonal and cyclical. These four patterns can be found together as well as each alone. A trend is said to exist when there is a pattern of growth or decline in the data over time. A horizontal pattern exists when the data are evenly distributed, i.e., when there is no obvious growth or decline in the data over time. Statistically, this is referred *to* as a stationary pattern. A seasonal pattern exists when a series fluctuates according to some seasonal factor. Lastly, a cyclical sub-pattern exists when there are fluctuations in data as a result of the general business cycle in the economy. This pattern is the most difficult pattern to predict as it does not repeat itself at constant intervals of time. In terms of suitability, simple exponential smoothing is more appropriate technique with horizontal sub-pattern in the data. In case of trend and seasonal data, higher torms of smoothing give good results. Decomposition technique of forecasting can adequately handle all combinations of horizontal, trend, seasonal and cyclical components. In case of horizontal, trend and seasonal patterns Box-Jenkins technique is useful. Cyclical and seasonal patterns can be handled well by multiple regression and econometric techniques- These techniques, however, should not be attempted when data sub-pattern is horizontal.

Data Requirement : The quantity and quality of data both are very important considerations in making choice of a forecasting technique. The data requirement differs from technique to technique. Causal model of forecasting requires more data in comparison with purely time series technique *of* forecasting. Therefore, causal techniques are more appropriate for medium and long term forecasting but not for short term forecasting. It is estimated roughly that simple exponential smoothing requires at least 10 observations; the decomposition, Box-Jenkins and multiple regression techniques require at least 30 observations; and econometric techniques require information mostly running into several hundred observations.

Number of Items : Number of items to be forecasted has a bearing on the type of forecasting technique to be selected and used. If the decision making process demands hundreds or even thousands of items to consider, then very simple technique of forecasting can be applied more or less in a mechanic fashion to each of the items so that equal number of forecasts are developed. If, on the other hand, single item is being forecast then one can afford the rigorous and more complex technique of forecasting.

Ease of Understanding and Application : This is quite a significant aspect in making choice of a forecasting technique to be adopted. A manager who prepares the forecast must also understand it. If the manager does not have high level of confidence in the prediction generated by forecasting technique, then it should not be used in the decision making process. That is the main reason that more advanced and sophisticated techniques of forecasting, such as econometric and input-output techniques, are not widely used. Undoubtedly, these techniques give very accurate forecasts, but prove to be complex for the ultimate user to understand the intricacies of the methods and one may not feel highly confident in these techniques. In terms of the ease of understanding and application, the ranking of the quantitative models from the easiest to the most difficult would be: simple exponential smoothing, decomposition, multiple regression, multivariate Box-Jenkins, and econometric techniques.

Cost: Cost aspect is yet another factor which needs attention. There are three elements of cost that are relevant in the application of a forecasting system. First, there is cost of developing the model. Obviously, this cost differs from technique to technique depending on the degree of simplicity or complexity of the model. Second is the cost of storing information and that too varies from technique to technique. There are some forecasting techniques which require the storage of very small amount of data, while other complex techniques require the storage of huge amount of data. Third is the cost of actual operation of the forecasting technique. The cost becomes tremendous when there are many items to be forecasted. On the basis of cost consideration, the quantitative techniques ranking from least costly to most costly are : Simple exponential smoothing, decomposition, multiple regression, Box-Jenkins, multivariate Box-Jenkins and econometric technique.

Accuracy : In majority of cases, accuracy is treated as the overriding criterion for selecting a forecasting technique. Accuracy implies as to what extent forecast figures approximate to the actual figures. The level of accuracy required will depend on the importance of the decision involved. For some decisions plus or minus 10 percent may do, but in other cases a variation of 2 percent could prove disastrous for the organization. It is very difficult to rank the forecasting methods in terms of the level of accuracy, as accuracy of a forecasting technique tends to differ from one situation to another. However, on the basis of the various studies available in this regard, it can be said that for immediate and short term forecasts, Box-Jenkins proves more accurate even than econometric model. Decomposition techniques of forecasting are relatively less accurate.

On the basis of the factors analyzed, in the matter of choosing a forecasting method, we may conclude as under. Select some feasible forecasting methods first taking into account the factors studied above and the characteristics of the situation. Then take a final decision after weighing forecasting cost against accuracy of the method. If a manager can use a more simple and less costly method and still achieves the required level of accuracy, be should go in for that technique. High cost method such as Box-Jenkins type can also be justified if the risk associated with forecasting errors are high. Generally, it would be wise to use less expensive and simple method of forecasting and then gradually to upgrade it to more sophisticated method. The tendency on the part of the manager to start with the most sophisticated and costly method may not yield rich dividend.

It must be pointed out at this place that what has been discussed in this section relates mostly to quantitative methods of forecasting. Unfortunately, it is not an easy task to assess the accuracy of qualitative methods as these are non-standardized procedures.

7.1.1 *Data Sources and other Data Aspects* : A major consideration in the selection of a forecasting method for a specific situation is the type of data available. Thus, the role of data is evident and pivotal in the development of any forecasting system. In case of quantitative forecasting techniques, data requirement is specific and immense. Therefore, a manager must be aware of the type of data required for developing a forecasting system. Data must be reliable, adequate and specific. We now deal with data source and some of the basic aspects relating to it.

Data Sources : There are three sources of data viz., existing accounting records, original data and published data. To collect data from the existing accounting records is the easiest and also the least costly. But the system is not without drawbacks. The major drawback is that the accounting system may be inflexible, thus necessitating the need to change its form suitably as per the requirement of the forecaster. Regarding original data, it is made available through survey technique. The chief advantage of original data is that it can be tailored to the specific needs of the manager in forecasting. But at the same time, this procedure of data collection is quite costly. Therefore, to gather data through published source in place of survey technique has increased quite rapidly during recent years. This reduces the cost of data collection. But the basic weakness of the published data lies in the fact that no information of the level of accuracy of such data is given. Unless accuracy of data is not determined, it is risky to use it for forecasting.

Data Aspects : It is absolutely necessary that the variables to be forecast are known and well defined. The variables which are crucial for forecasting need to be defined in terms of their following five aspects.

(i) *The Time Period Covered* : Though business is a continuous process but for accounting purposes it is necessary to define some period of time and to summarize the value of each variable for that time period. Long range forecasts must be based on observed historical data values for fairly long period of time such as bi-annually or annually. For immediate forecast aimed at controlling day-to day operations would require to be based on data values that cover a very short time such as an hour, one day etc.

(ii) *Levels of Details* : It is always most efficient to collect data at the most detailed level to the extent possible and then to aggregate it. To collect data at the aggregative level and then to break it down into minute details would be less efficient and less economical.

(iii) *The Frequency of Data*: The frequency of data is an important aspect. At what frequency level the data will be utilized? If it is known in advance then the data can be collected in the most efficient manner. For instance, if the forecast is to be made on the annual basis then there is hardly any need to collect the data at lower level. If it is to be applied for control then the data must be collected at a smaller interval say daily or twice a day or even hourly.

(iv) *The Unit of Measurement*: To determine appropriate unit is an important step in data collection. Generally, units are converted to some monetary units, say in rupees. But it is advisable to store the original units (raw data) before it is converted into another unit of measurement. This would also allow forecaster to go back to the raw data in order to perform various transformations. Not only this, it will save the forecaster from the loss of information which is likely to be there in most forecasting situations.

(v) *Required Level of Accuracy* : As pointed out earlier, the level of accuracy required would vary from one forecasting technique to another. It is an admitted fact that high level of accuracy can be introduced in forecasting with adequate data at higher cost. So it is essential that appropriate trade-off be made between the cost factor and level of accuracy.

7.1.2 *Management versus Forecaster:* There are many alternative forecasting techniques which indeed create the problem of managing the forecast that is to be chosen. A pre requisite for the effective management of a forecasting system is an appreciation of the role forecasting plays in management. Management and forecaster are the two important sets of persons for preparing and implementing a forecast. Forecaster prepares it while manager uses it. But the relations between the two are not always smooth, cordial and guaranteed. There may be some tension between management and the forecaster on several counts. The forecaster may feel that the management does not appreciate and makes insufficient use of the forecasts. On the other hand, managers may claim that the forecasts are not perfect and accurate and, therefore, cannot be used appropriately to the organization. This gap in communication can only be reduced when these two groups understand and respect each other's views. Management should have appreciation of the forecasting technique used. At the same time, the forecaster should be aware of the difficulties manager may face in implementing the forecast. Forecaster must also give indication clearly of the level of uncertainty attached to the figures and should resist the temptation to be completely optimistic in his prediction. Management should also be equally keen to supply with all the relevant information needed for the preparation of forecast and should not retain some information for his own use. Indeed, the basic important thing to be agreed upon by both sides is that they understand what is being forecast and why. If they do then it would enhance significantly the value of the organization's forecasting efforts.

Understandably, it is the responsibility of both the groups that good quality forecasts are generated. The forecaster must know the right type of data being used for forecasting. It is absolutely necessary that forecaster tends to keep up with new development in the field of forecasting. There is every need that management fosters congenial enviornment and facilities so that forecaster operates with all his tools in his kit very efficiently. This approach would significantly benefit the forecasting system like any other management task in the organization.

7.2 Forecasting as an Input to Planning

Forecasting is not done only for the sake of prediction but to convert it into an operating plan. A knowledge of forecasting is of no use unless it is effectively applied and integrated in the organization's planning process. Planning is the major use of forecasting. Because of the uncertainties in business which are likely to increase in foreseeable future rather the reverse, it has become increasingly essential to consider the future systematically in planning. In many industries, it has become necessary to think much farther ahead than ever before. For example, in aero-space and energy, a period of two or three decade is well within the scope of operational long term planning. The top management would like to see clearly what the future course of events would be. Thus, the need to forecast to help the planners in their decision making is evident. One or the other form of forecasting is essential for all future related planning. How the role of forecasting can be effectively integrated into the management and administrative tasks of planning and decision making can well be summarised as shown in Figure 7.1 suggested by Makridakis.

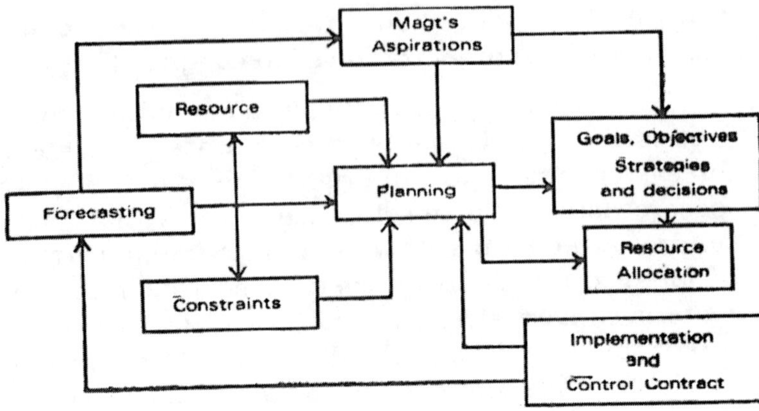

Fig. 7.1. Linking Forecasting with Planning and Decision Making.

It is brought out clearly from the Figure above that forecasting and planning which concern themselves with the future are the two important functions within the organization and can be linked and integrated. It is also evident that forecasting is associated with all the planning decisions.

But there are also critics who advocate that because of critical events which no reasonable man would have foreseen, forecasting can lead to inflexible planning. The answer to this criticism is that the major role of forecasting is not to provide definitive predictions of what will happen in the future but to clarify the future consequences of current development in the absence of unforeseen events and happenings. Systematic forecasting does help in a wide range of planning problems by (i) recording trends and factors which might otherwise have been ignored, and (ii) quantifying the probability and timing of future events.

However, it must be clearly understood that forecasting and planning are two distinct functions of management. The forecasting is only one of the essential inputs to planning. A forecast relates to a future state and is quite independent of the decisions of a particular organization. Contrary to it, planning is concerned with what a particular organization will attempt in the light of the information furnished by the forecast. But for obtaining good results and decisions both need to be integrated and linked.

7.3 Judgemental Factors in Forecasting

We have outlined in the earlier chapters various forecasting techniques both quantitative and qualitative. While preparing these formal forecasting techniques, human judgement which tends to play a very significant role, cannot be ignored. This is true, no matter, whatever technique is adopted for preparing forecast of any phenomenon. By all accounts human judgement must be incorporated to all the formal techniques of forecasting to generate a complete forecasting system. No doubt, making a judgement is not an easy process. This becomes very acute particularly when things are changing very fast due to science, economic fluctuations and unstable political climate inter-alia. It, however, does not mean that formal forecasts without judgement are never accurate. This is not the point, they are accurate in many situations. The relevant point is that beyond a certain period, the uncertainty factor which predominates cannot be determined correctly. To cover it up, judgemental factor needs to be incorporated in the main body of forecast. But unfortunate situation often remains is that judgemental factor is not taken very seriously in preparing quantitative forecasts. It would be desirable then to combine the good elements of judgement with formal forecasting system. To combine judgement to the formal forecasting is relatively a new area, yet some useful can be done if following suggestions are accepted and adhered to seriously.

The forecaster must have clear understanding of the relative advantages and disadvantages of each forecasting technique. For instance, quantitative techniques work excellently when the situation or the environment does not undergo a drastic change. But under the changed situations these techniques do not prove effective at all.

Keeping in view the problem faced above, it is quite logical to use quantitative techniques when no major changes in the environment are envisaged. But when there are such discerning changes then judgemental inputs should be given additional weight at an increasing rate. In order to generate a good forecast, when major changes do occur, the forecasting system should be monitored so as to signal to the need to change the relative emphasis to judgement and formal quantitative techniques in forecasting. Monitoring, in fact, should serve as warning system that continuously traces the fluctuations in variable which are non-random in character. This is an expanded role of forecasting system. Figure 7.2 illustrates this point.

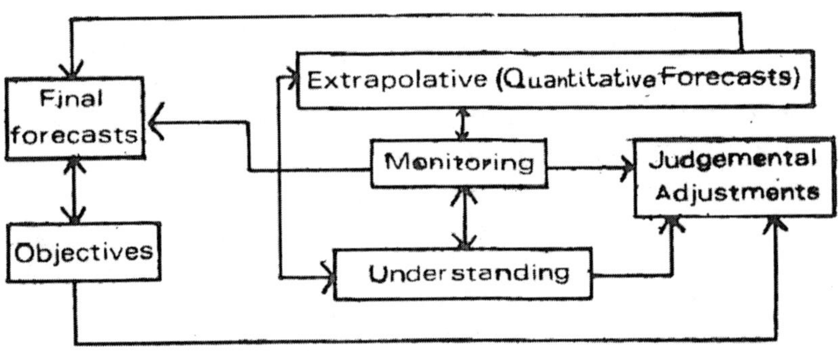

Fig. 7.2. Expanded Functions for Forecasting

Figure 7.2 suggests that forma! techniques should be adopted when there are random changes. If there are non-random changes then formal techniques should be modified as to combine the judgemental element. It is to be emphasized that formal techniques need not be changed unless the monitoring system gives a warning signal of a possible non-random change. Finally, for exploiting their advantages fully, forecaster must be knowledgeable enough so that the marriage between the judgemental input to quantitative technique is complete and goes off well.

7.4 The Role of Computer in Forecasting

Computer is quite a powerful and extremely useful tool for business management including forecasting. It performs the tasks faster, precisely and accurately. There are two aspects of the use of computer in forecasting. These two aspects are: mechanization capability and innovation. In its mechanization capability, the computer can perform three activities viz., volume processing, record keeping, computations and evaluations. These three activities can be performed by the computer without any loss of time. If the operation of these three activities is completely manual then it is not possible to take decision which requires immediate action.

Regarding the second aspect, i.e., innovative applications of the computer to modify the present technique of operation, many organizations do not attempt it. This is only to be attempted either by the most aggressive business firm or the most courageous executives. Many organizations are satisfied only upto the level of computer mechanization. The decision sounds wise as to go beyond computer mechanization into a more sophisticated area of forecasting is a very risky and expensive affair.

Despite the tremendous value of computer in forecasting only a very small number of organizations go in for computer. There are some difficulties in making use of computer in forecasting. Its prohibitive cost in forecasting is the first major hurdle. It is estimated that computer's cost is approximately 1.5 percent of sales. The second problem is to get experienced project management. Application of computer in forecasting requires programmer having knowledge of the total package of computer programme and also the services of fairly qualified statistician.

Fortunately, recently, a new type of computer package has been developed to support the manager in forecasting. These packages tend to cover a wide range of forecasting techniques. In addition to computer of all sizes, [now there are available programmable calculators making it possible for forecasters to programme their own forecasting routines. It is expected that hand held computers will be available very soon which can sufficiently support the forecasting function.

References and Select Bibliography

Almon, *C, et.al. Inter-industry Forecasts of the American Economy*. Lexington, Mass., Lexington Books, 1974.

American Management Association. *Materials and Methods of Sales Forecasting,* Special Report No. 27, New York, 1957.

Anderson, O. *Time Series Analysis and Forecasting: The Box-Jenkins Approach.* London, Butterworth, 1976.

Anderson, W.H.L. Forecasting Uses of Anticipatory Data, *Economic Journal,* June: 1958,

Angle, E. W. *Keys for Business Forecasting.* Federal Reserve Bank of Richmond, 1964.

Armstrong, J.S. *Long-Range Forecasting: From Crystal Ball to Computer.* New York: Wiley-Inter-Science, 1978.

Ascher, W. *Forecasting: An Appraisal for Policy Makers and Planners.* Baltimore: The Johns Hopkins University Press, 1978.

Bates, J.M. and Granger, C.W.J. Combination of Forecast, *Operational Research Quarterly,* 20 (4), 451-68, 1969.

Bhattacharya, M.N. Forecasting the Demand for Telephones in Australia, *Appl. Statist.,* 23, 1-10, 1974.

Blackman, A.W.A Cross Impact Model Applicable to Forecasts for Long-Range Planning, *Technological Forecasting and Social Change,* 5 (3), 253, 1973.

Box, G.E.P. and Jenkins, G.M. *Time Series Analysis, Forecasting and Control.* San Francisco: Holden Day, 1976.

Bratt, Elmer. *Buniness Cycles and Forecasting.* Homewood, 111: Richard D. Irwin, Inc., 1961.

Bratt, E.C. *Business Forecasting.* New York, McGraw Hill, Inc., 1958.

Bright, J. *Technology Forecasting—Concepts and Exercises.* Plma-quid Press, Austin, Texas, 1972.

Brown, R.G. *Smoothing Forecasting and Prediction of Discrete Time Series.* Englewood Cliffs, N.J. Prentice Hall, 1963.

Broida, Arthur. Diffusion Indexes, *The American Statistician,* June: 1955.

Butler, W.F. *(Ed.). How Business Economists Forecast,* Prentice-Hall, Inc., Englewood Cliffs, New Jersy, 1966.

Cantor, J. *Pragmatic Forecasting.* American Management Association, Inc., 1981.

Carter, Anne P. Technological Forecasting and Input-Output Analysis, *Technological Forecasting,* 1, 331-45, 1970.

Chambers, J.C. *et al.* How to Choose the Right Forecasting

Technique, *Harvard Business Review,* July-August: 1971.

Cohen, Merris. *Surveys and Forecasting, Methods and Techniques of Business Forecasting.* Englewood Cliffs, New Jersey Prentice- Hall, 1976.

Cowles, A. Can Stock Market Forecasters Forecast? *Econometriea,* 1 (3), 309-324, 1933.

Cramer, R. H. and Miller, R. B. Development of a Deposit Forecasting Procedure for use in Bank Financial Management, *Journal of Bank Research,* 4, 122-138, 1973.

Dalrymple, D. J. Sales Forecasting Methods and Accuracy, *Bush ness Horizons,* December: 1975.

De Hoogh, J. *et al.* Food for a Growing World Population, *Technological Forecasting and Social Change,* 10, 27-51, 1976.

Donovan, T.M.O, *Short-Term Forecasting.* New York, John Wiley & Sons, 1983.

Elliot-Jones, M. *Input-Output Analysis: A Non-technical Description,* Report 533. The Conference Board, 1971.

Fama, E. F. The Behaviour of Stock Market Prices, *Journal of Business,* 38 (1), 34-105, 1965.

Fischer, M. Towards a Mathematical Theory of Relevance Trees, *Technological Forecasting,* 1, 1970.

Forrester, Jay W. *World Dynamics.* Cambridge, Massachusetts, Wright-Allen Press, 1971.

Gabor, D. *Inventing the Future.* London, Seeker and Warburg, 1963.

George, Parker and Segura. How to Get a Better Forecast? *Harvard Business Review,* March April, 1971.

Gilchrist, W. *Statistical Forecasting.* London, Wiley, 1976.

Granger, C. W. J. and Newhold, P. *Forecasting Economic Time Series.* New York, Academic Press, 1976.

Granger, C. W. J. and Newhold, P. *Forecasting in Business and Economics.* Academic Press, 1976.

Gordon, T. J. and Hayward, H. Initial Experiments in the Cross Impact Method of Forecasting, *Futures,* 1 (2), 100, 1968.

Gorden, T. J. and Helmer, O. Report, P. The RAND Corporation, Santa Monica, California, Sep. 1964.

Harry, Jones and Brian C. Twiss. *Forecasting Technology for Planning Decisions.* London, The Macmillan Press Ltd., 1978.

Herman, O. Stekler. *Economic Forecasting.* New York: Prager, 1970.

Hogarth, R. M. and Makridakis, S. The Limits to Predictability, INSEAD Research Paper No. 133, 1982.

Holt, C. C. Forecasting Seasonal and Trends by Exponentially Weighted Moving Averages, Office of Naval Research, Memorandum No. 52, 1957.

Holt, C. C Forecasting and Planning: An Evaluation, *Management Science,* 27 (2), 1977.

Hymans, S. H. On the Use of Leading Indicators to Predict Cyclical Turning Points, Brookings Papers on Econometric Activity (2), 339-384, 1973.

Jantscb, E. *Technological Planning and Social Futures.* Cassell, 1972.

Kahn, H. *The Next 200 Years a Scenario for America and the World,* New York: Morrow, 1976.

Kahn, H. and Wiener, A. J. *The Year 2000: A Framework for Speculation on the Next Thirty Three Years.* The Hudson Institute, 1967.

Kahneman, D. and Tversky, A. Subjective Probability: A Judgement of Representativeness, *Cognitive Psychology,* 3 (3), 430-454, 1972.

Kahneman, D. and Tversky, A. On the Psychology of Prediction, *Psychological Review,* 80 (4), 237-51, 1973.

Klein, L. R. *An Essay on the Theory of Economic Prediction.* Chicago: Markham, 1971.

Leonard, S. Silk and Louise Curley M., *A Primer on Business Forecasting.* New York, Remdom House, 1970.

Leuthold, R. M., Mac Cormick, A. J. A., Schmitz, A. and Watts, D. G. Forecasting Daily Hog Prices and Qualities: A Study of Alternative Forecasting Techniques, *J.A.M. Statist. Association,* 65, 90-107, 1970.

Lewis, C. D. *Industrial and Business Forecasting Methods,* Butterworth, 1982.

Lin Stone, H. and Turoff, M. *The Delphi Method: Techniques and Applications.* Addison-Wesley, 1975.

Lorek, R. S., McDonald, C. L. and Patz, D. H. A Comparative Examination of Management Forecasts and Box Jenkins Forecasts of Earnings, *Accounting Review,* 51(2), 321-330, 1976.

Mabert, V. A. and Radcliffe, R. C. *A Forecasting Methodology as Applied to Financial Time Series,* 1974.

Macauley, F. R. *The Smoothing of Time Series,* National Bureau of Economic Research, 1930.

Machinery and Allied Products Institute. *Use of Input-Output Analysis as an Aid in Forcasting in the capital Goods Industries,* 1968.

Maiscl, S. J. *Fluctuations, Growth and Forecasting.* New York: John Wiley & Sons Inc., 1957.

Makridakis, S. *et al. Forecasting Methods and Applications,* New York, John Wiley & Sons, 1978.

Makridakis, S. and Hibon, M. Accuracy of Forecasting: An Empirical Investigation, *Journal Royal Statist. Society,* A-., 142(2)97-125, 1979.

Marbert, V.A. Statistical Versus Salei Force-Executive Opinion Short-Range Forecasts: A Time Series Analysis Case Study, *Decision Science,* 7, 310-318, 1976.

Martino, J. P. *Technological Farecasting for Decision Making,* New York, Amer., 1972.

Mazlish, B. *The Railroad and the Space Programme,* M. I. T. Press, 1965.

Meadows, D. H. *et al. The Limits to Growth,* New York: New Anler. Library, 1972.

Meadows, D. H. *et al. Dynamics of Growth in a Finite World.* Cambridge, Massachusetts; M. I. T. Press, 1974.

Meehl, P. E. *Clinical Versus Statistical Prediction: A Theoretical Analysis and Review of Literature,* Minneapolis University of Minnesota Press, 1954.

Miernyk, W. H. Long Range Forecasting with a Regional Input-Output Model, *Western Economic Journal,* VI, June: 1968.

Mitchell, W. C. *Business Cycles.* Berkeley, California, University of California Press, 1913.

Moore G. H. The Analysis of Economic Indicators, *Scientific American,* 232 January: 1975.

Nelson, C. R. *Applied Time Series Analysis and Managerial Fore-castings* San Francisco, Holden Day, 1973.

Nordhaus, W. D. World Dynamics: Measurement without Data, *Economic Journal,* 83, 1156-1183. 1973.

O' Carroll, F. M. Subjective Probabilities and Short-Term Economic Forecasts: An Empirical Investigation, *Appl. Statist,* 26 (3) 269-78, 1977.

O' Connor, W. J. A Methodology for Analogies, *Journal of Technological Forecasting and Social Change,* 2-3 (4), 289, 1971.

Osborn, A. *Your Creative Power and Applied Imagination Scribner,* New York, 1963.

OsKamp, S. Over-confidence in Case-Study Judgments, *J. Consulting Psychology,* 29 (3), 261-65, 1965.

Pegels, C. C. Exponential Forecasting: Some New Variations, *Management Science,* 12 (5), 311-315 1969.

Reid, D. J. *Forecasting in Action: A Comparison of Forecasting Techniques in Economic Time Series,* Proceedings of the Joint Conference of the Operations Research Society, Long-Range Planning and Forecasting, 1971.

Roger, K. Chisholm, Gilbert, R. Whitaker. *Forecasting Methods,* Homewood 111. Richard D. Irwin, 1971.

Roos, Charles F. Survey of Economic Forecasting Techniques, *Econometrica,* Oct.: 1955.

Rubin Field, D. L. *Econometric Models and Economic Forecasts,* Mcgraw Hill, New York, 1976.

Shiskin, J. and Lampart, L. H. Indicator Forecasting. In. *Methods and Techniques of Business Forecasting,* Englewood Cliff, New Jersy, Prentice Hall, 1976.

Shiskin, J. *Electronic Computers and Business Indicators.* National Bureau of Economic Research, Occasional Paper 57, 1957.

Shiskin, J. *et al.* The X-ll Variant of the Census II Method Seasonal Adjustment Programme, Bureau of the Census Technical Paper No. 15.

Slutzky, E. The Summation of Random Causes as the Source of Cyclic Process. *Econometrica,* 5, 105-46, 1937.

Stanford Research Institute. *Handbook of Forecasting Techniques.* S. R. I., 1975.

Stckler, H. O. Forecasting with Econometric Models. An Evaluation, *Econometrica,* 36, July-October, 1968.

Steckler, O. and Schepsman M. Forecasting with an Index of Leading Series, *Journal of the American Statistical Association,* 68, 291-95, 1973.

Sussex Science Policy Research Unit. Malthus with a Computer, *Futures,* 5, 1973.

Theil, Henri. *Economic Forecasts and Policies.* American Elsevier Publishing Company, New York, 1975.

Thomopoulos, N.T. *Applied Forecasting Methods,* Prentice-Hall, Englewood Cliffs, New Jersy, 1980.

Tobin, J. On the Predictive Value of Consumer Intentions and Attitudes, *Review of Economics and Statistics,* August: 1959.

Trigg, D. W. Monitoring a Forecasting System, *Operational Research Quarterly,* 15, 271-74, 1964.

U.S. Govt. *Business Conditions Digest.* Washington D. C. (monthly published).

Vigderhous. G. Forecasting Sociological Phenomenon: Application of Box-Jenkins Methodology to Suicide Rates. In: K.F. Schuessler (ed.), *Sociological Methodology,* Jossey-Bass, San Franscisco, 20-51, 1978,

Wheelwright. S.C. and Darral G.C. Corporate Forecasting: Promise and Reality, *Harvard Business Review,* Nov.-Dec; 1976.

Winters, P.R. Forecasting Sales by Exponentially Weighted Moving Averages, *Management Science,* 6, 324-342, 1960.

Wold, H. *A Study in the Analyses of Stationary Time Series.* Stockholm: Almquist & Wiksell (1st ed., 1938), 1954.

Wright, P. The Harassed Decision Maker: Time Pressures, Distractions and the Use of Evidence, *Journal of Applied Psychology,* 59 (5), 555-61, 1974.

Zwicky, F. Morphology of Propulsive Power. Monographs on Morphological Research, No. 1. Pasadena, Calif: Society of Morphological Research, 1962.

Index

P

Q

R

S

T

U

V

W

Y

Z